Natural Process

An Anthology of New Black Poetry

Edited by <u>Ted Wilentz</u> and Tom Weatherly

 Hill and Wang • New York

THE EDITORS OF THIS ANTHOLOGY are grateful to the poets themselves for permission to publish their poems. In some cases poems in this volume originally appeared in books or magazines. Acknowledgment is made to the following:

The Antioch Review, for William J. Harris' "For Bill Hawkins, A Black Militant."

Black Dialogue, for Al Young's "Friday the Twelfth."

Broadside Press, for Nikki Giovanni's "Knoxville, Tennessee," "Nikki-Rosa," and "For Saundra," from *Black Judgement*, copyright © 1968 by Nikki Giovanni. Also for Nikki Giovanni's "Adulthood," "Seduction," "Wilmington Delaware," and "My Poem," from *Black Feeling, Black Talk*, copyright © 1968 by Nikki Giovanni.

Carolina Quarterly, for Michael S. Harper's "Ode to Tenochtitlan."

Chicago Review, for Al Young's "Everywhere."

Corinth Books, for Tom Weatherly's "pool doos paid," "mud water shango," "red & yellow fooles coat," "blues for franks wooten," and "tomcat," from *Maumau American Cantos*, copyright © 1970 by Tom Weatherly.

The Lit, for Al Young's "The Curative Powers of Silence."

Mad River Review, for William J. Harris' "A Winter Song."

Moore Publishing Company, for William J. Harris' "With My Napalm Six Shooters" and "Samantha Is My Negro Cat," from *Nine Black Poets*, copyright © 1969 by Moore Publishing Company.

Negro Digest, for Michael S. Harper's "Effendi."

New American Review, for Jay Wright's "The Homecoming Singer" and "Wednesday Night Prayer Meeting."

Poetry (Chicago), for Michael S. Harper's "The Black Angel" and "New Season."

Poetry Northwest, for Michael S. Harper's "Proposition 15" and "Aftermath"; and Jay Wright's "The Invention of a Garden" and "Moving To Wake at Six."

Quarterly Review of Literature, for Michael S. Harper's "We Assume."

Third World Press, for Carolyn M. Rodgers' "Plagiarism for a Trite Love Poem," "U Name This One," "Jesus Was Crucified or It Must Be Deep," and "It Is Deep,' from *Songs of a Blackbird*, copyright © 1969 by Carolyn M. Rodgers.

23 California Poets (Ante-Echo Press), for Al Young's "Lonesome in the Country."

Contents

Natural Process *v*

Introduction *viii*

CONYUS *1*
Black Moses   He's doing natural life   a day in the life of . . .
December Twenty-Six 1968   For Che   requiem for tomorrow
Mama Too Tight

SAM CORNISH *14*
Sam's World   Montgomery   One Eyed Black Man in Nebraska
Courting   Cross over the River   Lord   Other Nat Turners
Frederick Douglass

NIKKI GIOVANNI *21*
Knoxville, Tennessee   Nikki-Rosa   Adulthood   Seduction
Wilmington Delaware   For Saundra   My Poem

MICHAEL S. HARPER *32*
Proposition 15   Black Study   Ode to Tenochtitlan   Effendi
Where Is My Woman Now   Aftermath   The Black Angel
We Assume   Another Season   New Season

WILLIAM J. HARRIS *44*
My Friend, Wendell Berry   With My Napalm Six Shooters
We Live in a Cage   I, Satan   For Bill Hawkins, A Black Militant
Samantha Is My Negro Cat   Habitual   A Winter Song   Can
I Write You an Anthem

DAVID HENDERSON *54*
Poem for Painters

AUDRE LORDE *65*
Naturally   Fantasy and Conversation   The Woman Thing
7/2   And What about the Children   Rites of Passage
Bloodbirth   The American Cancer Society   A Poem for a Poet

L. V. MACK *76*
Mad Man's Blues   Over a Glass of Wine   Biafra
Zeus in August   Piece   Death Songs   Jungle Fever

CLARENCE MAJOR *84*
In Chapala, Jal   Is Natural, Takes Me In   Guadalajara   Weak
Dynamite   Pictures   Dynamite Transported from Canada to
New York City   How to Describe Fall from Now On

N. H. PRITCHARD   *92*
Concrete Poems

LENNOX RAPHAEL   *99*
Mike 65   Nightime

CAROLYN M. RODGERS   *111*
Portrait   We Dance Like Ella Riffs   The Rain Is in Our Heads
c. c. rider   Plagiarism for a Trite Love Poem   U Name This
One   Jesus Was Crucified   It Is Deep

SONIA SANCHEZ   *124*
right on: white america   for our lady   summer words for a
sister addict   so this is our revolution   blk / rhetoric
answer to yr / question   indianapolis

ASKIA MUHAMMAD TOURÉ   *134*
JuJu   Pome for Dionne Warwick aboard the aircraft carrier,
U.S.S. Enterprise   Tauhid

TOM WEATHERLY   *143*
arroyo   crazy what she calls   for billie   pool doos paid
mud water shango   red & yellow fooles coat
blues for franks wooten   speculum oris

JAY WRIGHT   *150*
An Invitation to Madison County   Moving to Wake at Six
The Homecoming Singer   Wednesday Night Prayer Meeting
The Invention of a Garden

AL YOUNG   *167*
The Song Turning Back into Itself   Lonesome in the Country
Everywhere   Malagueña Salerosa   The Kiss   There Is a Sadness
Ponce De León / a Morning Walk   Dear Old Stockholm
The Curative Powers of Silence   Friday the Twelfth

iv

Natural Process

From the dark continent of the European
mind (commerce), across the blue middle
passage to Jong sang doo, to straddle big muddy,
east up the coast, we sing bad mouf songs
for real love within our lives.

We turn fast corners wif magic feets this year.

(The Scottsboro buck.)
On clear Saturdays read Langston Hughes,
make my bed, off to dig on Tarzan, king of great apes,
swinging down by head at the Ritz. Langston
and Tarzan fight cold war for my soul flesh,
and I spend out high school, my allowance, hanging
wif the rest of the niggers in the balcony. The *man*
on the screen, swinging through the trees,
beating the shit out the natives. Ignorant Africans!
I don't have the withal to argue this complement, eating baloney,
sitting wif my uncle John Will, the champeen shucker
of Jackson and Madison Counties. He has a chicken fat
imagination, and as champ chicken plucker of Jackson
County knew who is getting plucked. Hmmmm, the Africans
have more gumption than the local shines, niggers up
there in the U.N. dressing like Winston Churchill
wif war and a piece.
                              Afroamerican poets writing in stony
new English, or knightly, clannish y'all syrup. I say
I'm gonna figure up a language for all Americans (heh!),
the language I'll use as an *American* poet, colored and
charming. There ain't many differences between Jupiter
Hammon and Moon Mullins, and we all got it brothers,
bible tracts in the arm, numb to the inevitable.
                              Writing
English doggerel is a bitch, you conceit, pick
up pen write love sonnets to nine numb bitches.

(The Atlanta brave.)
  The student non-violent committed
sit-in for lunch at the Billy Club, and feel
language in action. Mister Crab having hard thots
on them honking our music cracking our skulls.
We kick back beginning now. Heavy sole under this shine.
Kicking Buck Benny's dues I pay in early admission
to soul mother Morehouse, she still putting out
Negro Men—pride of the South. Or in a Normal,
Alabama school, James Vinson rapping Chaucer round my ears,
while the administration suspends me for publishing
on campus without permission. I have enuf Bama,
Bull Connor getting his nuts in the street
putting down niggers. There is no chance of Chaucer
or Connor conking my head. Yeh yeh you know all.
I know, but we don't live in the same medium.
I know the schools: San Francisco, Black Mountain
New York, Beat, LeRoi Jones. BLAHBLAH THE FIFTYS
A TURBULENT AND CREATIVE PERIOD IN
 AMERICAN LETTERS.
Lissen to these new fresh young poets liberate poesy from form,
ideas, and ideology; like Charles Olson, they don't write in
 broken,
poverty-stricken English. They don't howl
at the moon inside the jacket of their anthology.
DIPSHIT PACK-HALL-SIMPSON they all cry, wolf,
wolf, at the door.
      I'm here to shuck your ears
'way from precise new English, to turn you 'round
to telling the down truth, law! Brothers, sisters,
I introduce you to, for the most
part, new acquaintances, brothers and sisters who set
down on paper flesh poems and poems that cut
like a hawk razor.
      You can't shuffle the words
out, believe that now, you all can't carry
razors anyhow Miss Ann, even like a washwoman.

You shuffle razors, baby, cut your self.

We turn fast corners wif magic feets this year.
Hmmmm, AfroAmerican Art is selling
at higher prices this year, hardtime head getting higher
each year, inflates
hard times in my economy, mebbe yours too.
    We do an anthology, no literary debts to pay, or dues,
a crack historian and a back home singer.
The poets and poems we could just compromise on
are not in here.
    LeRoi/Amer is not the father of modern Afro
American poetry, tho I feel the spirit to move
that heavy appellation on 'im. We look over his shoulder,
'timidating him, electing him to cry Baaaaa
in the wilderness, black magic, a pool doo telling us
it is our own.
                Ameer Baraka, mouf wide open,
what you got to say is valuable, you cannot
repudiate your earlier poems, they are there;
America can't resist your today
poems, here is what they may have inspired. Here are
your brothers, sisters, sons and daughters,
collected to replace the King James gang version.

                                    TOM WEATHERLY   1970

vii

Introduction

WHEN ARTHUR WANG asked me to edit an anthology of young black poets, I knew I would like to do such a collection if I could go to the writers for fresh work rather than to publishers for material that was easily available. In today's situation, this would be a problem for a white editor. More important was that while my involvement with contemporary poets and poetry seemed meaningful for the proposed book, it also made me aware that my white background placed limits on that knowledge. The idea of the anthology was too exciting not to look for an answer to these difficulties—a young, black co-editor whose knowledge and relationships would complement mine. I had been working with Tom Weatherly, editing the *Maumau American Cantos*. A mutual respect had developed with the happy feeling that we stimulated each other. When I asked if he would be a co-editor of this book, he enthusiastically agreed.

Before asking Tom, I had thought out another basic problem. Were there sufficient reasons for a selection of black poets rather than an "integrated" anthology? The existence of this collection makes the decision obvious. Whether or not we believe blacks are born separate, or should achieve separateness, there is no question that separateness has been thrust upon them. This has led to an ignorance of black achievements that extends to editors and publishers and is abetted by the fact that many of the new black magazines and books cannot be found unless you visit black bookstores like Mores's and Marcus' in San Francisco, Ellis' in Chicago, Memorial in New York, and Drum and Spear in Washington.

Hopefully, an anthology like the present one will help reduce this lack of communication. It should also show the variety, energy, and talent burgeoning among blacks. The work songs, gospels, and blues that have contributed so much to American poetry show the great potential that exists among people with a strong verbal tradition. The potential was not realized because a forcibly enslaved and uneducated group could not produce much in an art form as complex and as demanding of education and a written tradition as poetry.

Poetry is a compressed expression of beliefs, feelings and forms that comes out of a tradition and culture and out of a personal experience and nature. A personal nature is an individual quality, however it is shaped by life. Black Americans share the tradition and culture of white Americans, but the black and white experiences are different. For this reason, contemporary black poetry has its own quality. The emphasis on word play, for example, is surprising. It may stem partly from an African heritage. It may also come from the days of slavery, when subtle verbal communication was necessary, and messages regarding plots were passed on in speech and song.

There are differences between black and white poetry in themes and language. At a time when young whites are influenced by Olson's American myth, O'Hara's personism and Ginsberg's apocalyptic religiosity, young black poets are strongly affected by the militant movement, the pressure to be functional as a "steel cable." In their writings are references deriving from a black American experience. This is an experience that knows the meaning of "the dozens" and "double mojo"; that looks on drugs as a killing fact of life, not as a key to mystical experiences or an experiment in expanding consciousness; that understands why black women are not likely to join the women's liberation movement; that can tell you why almost every black poet has written to Trane. This experience can lead to magazines so full of "hate whitey" lines that it is an exercise in masochism for a white man to read them. Look at *Black Dialogue*, *The Journal of Black Poetry* and *Nommo*; then turn to *Poetry*, *The World* and *Stony Brook*. There exist two worlds in America. This division of consciousness is reflected in this anthology. We have also tried to show the different concerns of black poets and the wide variety, ranging from the rhythms and long lines of Askia Muhammed Touré to the concrete poetry of N. H. Pritchard.

Although these poems are in an all-black collection, any of them could be included in a general anthology since cultural pluralism is part of the American tradition. It is significant that LeRoi Jones, the dominant figure in black literature today, made a reputation as a writer, editor, and publisher with color a minor factor. In the twenties, Countee Cullen and others met at The Dark Tower, their informal club in Harlem, and lamented that they were considered Negro poets instead of poets. Jones, on the other hand, was part of a group of artists and writers that included De Kooning, O'Hara, and Ginsberg. They met, not in Harlem, but at Greenwich Village's Cedar Tavern. Jones's own work, his *Yūgen* magazine, and his Totem books played meaningful parts in the rejuvenation of poetry in the fifties and early sixties. Deservedly, he was in Don Allen's landmark 1960 anthology, *The New American Poetry*.

The present selection is intended to show what has happened since the breakthrough of the "new American poetry" and since Jones gained his reputation. It indicates there will be many good black poets instead of the thin line of reserves behind the Harlem Renaissance. That there is a separation of the poets, "the antennae of the race," that there is such hostility to whites, warn us that a great deal must be done to repair great social injustices. Otherwise we will have more people declaring like Langston Hughes, "America never was America to me."

This is a time of great mobility, and writers are more peripatetic than most. We could never track down a few, and a few more never answered our letters. Clarence Major has consoled me with the fact that one fourth of the poets he asked to be in his important *New Black Poets* never responded. We regret that some writers we admire are not represented. We are pleased by the quality of those who are and delighted that for several of the poets this is their first appearance in book form.

I would like to thank the editors and publishers of "little presses" who help show what is happening and help it happen. Joe Gonsalves deserves particular mention for his *Journal of Black Poetry*, even though I disagree with its views. My appreciation to Al Young and to Carolyn Weatherly for their aid. Last, but not least, I would like to mention my wife, Joan, whose comments and criticism and patience have all played their part in the working out of *Natural Process*.

September 1970   TED WILENTZ

Conyus

Black Moses
                     Black Moses
Black Moses
                  Black

he laid
on the asphalt
porch   blood
spurting from
the open wound

all around
him and someone
cried, "Oh My God!
Oh My God!"

people yelling
everywhere pointing
fingers at
vacant spots
where shadows
move into the
fusion of sirens
& flashing red
lights

the air dead
—and still
whispering love
& its poisonous
enzyme stirring

he moved ever
so lightly
"Oh My God!"
& his last breath
escaped into
the kaleidoscope
of faces
        bleeding
from his
mouth   nose
throat warm
blood soaking
into the cold
pavement

the wind took
his breath
& cast it back
into the vermilion
pond of non
violence

on this truth
ful day in
memphis tenn.
brothers
& sisters
around the
world
hearing

2

the news of
his death,
getting it
together to
give back
to them

do rags removed
straightening iron
put away
dinners left
uncooked

running through
the streets
burning   looting
busting heads
running it
down about
how

we have to
fuck up
now with
him gone
cause

man like
he sho'
ain't go
rise on easter
& it's about
time to
fuck up any
way anyhow
they said on
south fifth
& third,

"Oh My God!"
& kicked the motherfucking window
in

He's doing natural life

for Roy

behind his dinner jacket
smiling at the white wait
ers

revealing his half straight
ass hair in the light so
they wldn't detect his

defection from harlem
or his blk mama

using the right spoon
& fork placing the nap
kin just so that it
caught all the garbage

waving his little finger
behind his coffee cup
like a diploma from fisk

displaying excellent ill
usions of etiquette in the
leather chair with a cigar

between his narrow mustache
& a middle class pouch
dangling over his belt

4

doing research for the feds
on the negro problem with
subsidized funds from blk

lynching or fumes from birming
ham churches going up in flame

like tidbits of flesh
or pink pacifiers

fed to hungry lions

or eloquent darkies

dining at the white house

a day in the life of ...

i've been in an open field
for ten days or more,
a field of wheat & small children.

birds float lazily over-head
suspended in transparent
images of precision, the

day like whispering passion
moves a spanish wind
(rewinding itself across
     hillsides into obsession.

i come here often
pass the town of swollen
bodies, the river of blood
the faces of stoic flesh,

the crimson moon hiding,
the guilty fingers
of imperialist accusations.

back there
in the town
of musty diversion
they have locked their
doors with fear, closed
their coffins with death,
passed through operas with war,
moved
across strands of
violins with
fingers of death

trailing traces of broken
liberations.

here as in all
pagodas umber
chimes poem in
the wind.

(we never talk
   the children increase

with truth in their eyes
like mellow   distribution
of happiness birds fly
watching the seasons vanish

into the winter hills
like cotton fingers
caressing the black breast
of Jezebel.

December Twenty-Six 1968

The truce now over
For the twenty-four
Hour period, they begin
To kill again in the dawn
Smoke rising above the
Rice fields.
Vietnamese children
Lay sprawled below
The branches of xmas
Trees, wrapped in fear
& hunger, a bargain gift
From a wealthy uncle,
The day after
The big sale.

For Che

They hate you Che,
       Your picture hangs in Wash. next to Johnson's

They love you Che,
       Tears flowing from their eyes, when they heard
       of your death

They buried you Che,
       In gothic libraries of New York

They discovered you Che,
       Living incognito in the Vatican

They hear you Che,
       Laughing in the walls of the pentagon

7

They idolize you Che,
>In the university plotting revolution

They read you Che,
>In the White House & Kremlin with fear

They exploit you Che,
>In intellectual circles, using your name

They want you Che,
>To dance with Lady Bird

They watch you Che,
>Disassemble petrified forests of ideology

They recognize you Che,
>Destitute   black forgotten angels

They remember you Che,
>Beneath the "El" in Chicago

They hide you Che,
>In the folded caverns of their heart

They cry for you Che,
>At night beneath the quivering thighs of lovers

They ask for you Che,
>At receptions for foreign diplomats

They immortalize you Che,
>On toilet walls with dead prophets

They canonize you Che,
>With tongues of Yakut poets

They arrested you Che,
>Hitch-hiking through Texas

They watch you Che,
>Hording loot on t.v. riots

8

They patrol you Che,
        Throughout every ghetto in the world

They despised you Che,
        Not wanting to see themselves

They look for you Che,
        When-ever they see a beard, or saint

They hate you Che,
        In business grey and martini magic

They'll help you Che,
        Burned out bodies of napalm babies

They understood you Che,
        Lumumba, Malcolm, Ho Chi Minh

We suffer with you Che,
        In the prisons and jails of sorrow

They want you Che,
        To confess to playing god

They remembered you Che,
        In distortive harbors of Cuba

They rob you Che,
        Of all that's holy and sacred

They know Che,
        You haven't died, only regrouped
        your forces & surrounded hell

We love you Che,
        In cold water flats   with cocaine eyes
        and baster children

They're talking of you now Che,
        About the revolution you ignited
        & your similarities to their christ,

Then hurry home, to copulate with catholic penises
       & nine months later

Belch bombs from the wombs of their plastic women

requiem for tomorrow

there aren't any
apparitions today
the room is full
of windows
i can see the
holes

seven times
i put my
hand against
the pane to
touch the cool
objects passing

there is nothing
left but only lean
winds that glide
through their
motions   i can
see the holes
the day

filled with
gaunt gestures
the hours
strained
through bone
& marrow

there is nothing
expected
nor
leaving

Mama Too Tight

for Archie Schepp

(*Taken from the title
of the album* Mama
Too Tight *by Archie
Schepp*)

like all these
cats fell out
of the pool room
when this fine sister
walked by in
a short tight
skirt swinging
all her monthly
endowments in
classic motion
from street to

curb   stopping
traffic and business
as she passed in
undulating rhythm
making music,
Rufus turned
to Sonny Boy

watching her
& said,
"Blow!
You Motherfucker
Blow!"

CONYUS

"Born: CONYUS
          November 2, 1942
          Detroit, Michigan
Has traveled / Has LoVed ? / Has Hurt. / Has been HuRt
Presently being held in exile by one of our far western states."

"no compromise
     collective
black
     functional
black
     documentary
no
     compromising
blk
     for copper
contraband
     established
literature
     unless
we
     decide
to
     burn
it
     with
blk
     music
black
     art
& poems
     that
breathe

direction"

EDITORS' NOTE: Conyus is now out of prison on parole.

Sam Cornish

Sam's World

sam's mother has
grey combed hair

she will never touch
it with a hot iron

she leaves it
the way the lord
intended

she wears it proudly
a black and grey
round head of hair

Montgomery

for rosa parks

white woman have you heard
she is too tired to sit in the back
her feet two hundred years old

move to the back or walk
around to the side door how
long can a woman be a cow

your feet will not move
and you never listen
but even if it rains empty
seats will ride through town

i walk for my children
my feet two hundred years old

One Eyed Black Man in Nebraska

The skin quickens to noises.
The ground beneath a black man opens.

His wife in her nightgown
hears horses and men in her husband's
deathbed.

White horses move through the fields
lifting men out of darkness.

In the pillows, she keeps
a rifle and twenty two,
for hunting rabbits and keeping alive.

Still he dies,
one eye closed on the ground.

Courting

i am tall
          my hands are

ready   &

when i want

a woman

               to see   me

i   dress in white

and   black women

        turn and see my face

                              it is darker
and memorable
                       when   i
pass
      through the plantation

Cross over the River

harriet tubman
coming down the river
black face
reflected in the water

harriet tubman
in a gunboat
singing

slaves on the shore
singing
there is a home   somewhere

Lord

Lord,
        when I think
of your hands
                        my milk
shake
        gets warms,
and I
want to stay
                with the poor
and go into their
                        shacks.

When I see your crown,
and know you have suffered

for us,
    I sit on these dark
chairs.
        The smoke of coal
fires and bodies;
             are those
of your world also,
              these dark people.

        I want
to help them lord,
           with prayer,
patience,
        and night school
classes,
        and maybe someday
they'll be middle class

and drink of your blood

and eat
        of your body.

Other Nat Turners

      george washington
was for the rights
          of man
  sent his men
        to stop his niggers
  from sailing
        on british ships

phillis wheatley
                  black in skin
    half white in mind
                        read the bible
      went to god and poetry
wrote a poem
                for the good general george
      kept away from the fields
and slavery
                she had a silence
and another country
                        his life touched hers
    like skin
            afraid of its shadow

Frederick Douglass

my mother twice in her life on worn feet
walked an afternoon against the southern
heat to bring me a ginger cake
her face lined with scars in wrinkled
skin was only twenty three

my mother carried me in the fields and slept
on black ground as i turned within our skin
and as a child white fingers walked into her
mouth to count the teeth and raise the price

i was born somewhere between the shacks
and evenings when shadows were tired across
the fields and dresses grey with dust

SAM CORNISH: "I am thirty-three years old, have lived in Balti-more most of my life except for 1967–68 when I was in Boston, Mass. My jobs have been plentiful and varied—from door-to-door salesman to educational consultant.

"My professional experience: editor and publisher of *Mimeo*, a small magazine of poetry; editor of *Chicory*, a magazine of inner-city writing that is now under contract to the Associated Press; publisher of Cambridge Poetry Series, which consists of small books of poems by individual poets.

"By 1966, four books of my own poetry had appeared: *Generations, Angels, In This Corner,* and *People Under the Window.* In 1967, I was awarded a grant of $1,500 by the National Council for the Arts and also had *Winters,* a book of poetry, published by the Sans Souci Press in Cambridge, Massachusetts.

"In 1968 I appeared in two anthologies of poetry, *Black Fire*, edited by LeRoi Jones and Larry Neal, and *New Black Poetry*, edited by Clarence Major.

"In 1969, a children's book, *Sam,* was accepted by Harcourt, Brace and World Publishing Company. Three manuscripts are under consideration by different publishers.

"I have been widely published in small poetry magazines all over the country and have given a number of readings at such places as Harvard University, Johns Hopkins University, the University of Kentucky, and the Village Gate in New York.

"This coming year (1970) I have been asked to read at colleges and universities in Michigan and Ohio, and I will also be one of the group of poets reading on the New England Poetry Circuit."

"I am not a guy with a whole lot to say about poetry, except that I like it and feel some of the best modern poetry is to be found in the films of John Ford, Richard Lester, and Samuel Peckinpaw. I can also add the film music of Bernard Herman, Jerry Goldsmith, Elmer Bernstein, and the voice of Judy Collins. Poets I admire are William Stafford, Robert Bly, Jay Wright, and Emmett Jarrett—sometimes Robert Hershon and Duane Locke."

Nikki Giovanni

Knoxville, Tennessee

I always like summer
best
you can eat fresh corn
from daddy's garden
and okra
and greens
and cabbage
and lots of
barbecue
and buttermilk
and homemade ice-cream
at the church picnic
and listen to
gospel music
outside
at the church
homecoming
and go to the mountains with
your grandmother
and go barefooted
and be warm
all the time
not only when you go to bed
and sleep

Nikki-Rosa

childhood remembrances are always a drag
if you're Black
you always remember things like living in Woodlawn
with no inside toilet
and if you become famous or something
they never talk about how happy you were to have your mother
all to yourself and
how good the water felt when you got your bath from one of
    those
big tubs that folk in chicago barbecue in
and somehow when you talk about home
it never gets across how much you
understood their feelings
as the whole family attended meetings about Hollydale
and even though you remember
your biographers never understand
your father's pain as he sells his stock
and another dream goes
and though you're poor it isn't poverty that
concerns you
and though they fought a lot
it isn't your father's drinking that makes any difference
but only that everybody is together and you
and your sister have happy birthdays and very good christmasses
and I really hope no white person ever has cause to write about
    me
because they never understand Black love is Black wealth and
    they'll
probably talk about my hard childhood and never understand
    that
all the while I was quite happy

Adulthood

for claudia

i usta wonder who i'd be

when i was a little girl in indianapolis
sitting on doctors porches with post-dawn pre-debs
(wondering would my aunt drag me to church sunday)
i was meaningless
and i wondered if life
would give me a chance to mean

i found a new life in the withdrawal from all things
not like my image

when i was a teen-ager i usta sit
on front steps conversing
the gym teachers son with embryonic eyes
about the essential essence of the universe
(and other bullshit stuff)
recognizing the basic powerlessness of me

but then i went to college where i learned
that just because everything i was was unreal
i could be real and not just real through withdrawal
into emotional crosshairs or colored bourgeoisie intellectual
    pretensions
but from involvement with things approaching reality
i could possibly have a life

so catatonic emotions and time wasting sex games
were replaced with functioning commitments to logic and
necessity and the gray area was slowly darkened into
a black thing

for a while progress was being made along with a certain degree
of happiness cause i wrote a book and found a love
and organized a theatre and even gave some lectures on
Black history
and began to believe all good people could get
together and win without bloodshed
then
hammarskjold was killed
and lumumba was killed
and diem was killed
and kennedy was killed
and malcolm was killed
and evers was killed
and schwerner, chaney and goodman were killed
and liuzzo was killed
and stokely fled the country
and le roi was arrested
and rap was arrested
and pollard, thompson and cooper were killed
and king was killed
and kennedy was killed
and i sometimes wonder why i didn't become a debutante
sitting on porches, going to church all the time, wondering
is my eye make-up on straight
or a withdrawn discoursing on the stars and moon
instead of a for real Black person who must now feel
and inflict
pain

Seduction

one day
you gonna walk in this house
and i'm gonna have on a long African
gown
you'll sit down and say "The Black . . . "
and i'm gonna take one arm out
then you—not noticing me at all—will say "What about this
    brother . . . "
and i'm going to be slipping it over my head
and you'll rapp on about "The revolution . . . "
while i rest your hand against my stomach
you'll go on—as you always do—saying "I just can't dig . . . "
while i'm moving your hand up and down
and i'll be taking your dashiki off
then you'll say "What we really need . . . "
and i'll be licking your arm
and "The way I see it we ought to . . . "
and unbuckling your pants
"And what about the situation . . . "
and taking your shorts off
then you'll notice
your state of undress
and knowing you you'll just say
"Nikki,
isn't this counterrevolutionary . . . ?"

Wilmington Delaware

Wilmington is a funni negro
He's a cute little gingerbread man who stuffs his pipe with
Smog and gass fumes and maybe (if you promise not to tale)
just a little bit of . . . pot
Because he has to meet his maker each and everyday
LORD KNOWS HE'S A GOOD BOY AND TRIES HARD
While most of us have to go to church only once a week

They tell me he's up for the coloredman of the year award
And he'll probably win
(If he'd just stop wetting on himself each and everytime he
meets a Due-pontee)
LORD KNOWS HE TRIES

Why just the other day I heard him say NO
But he was only talking to the janitor and I believe they
expect him to exercise some control over the excreationary
facilities around here
(But it's a start)

My only real criticism is that he eats his daily nurishment at
    the "Y"
And I was taught that's not proper to do in public

But he's sharp, my but that boy is sharp
Why it took the overlords two generations to recognize that
    negroes
had moved to the East side of town (which is similar to but not
    the same as the wrong side of the tracks)
And here he is making plans for future whites who haven't even
reclaimed the best land yet

"Don't say nothing Black or colored or look unhappy"
I heard him tell his chief joints . . .
And every bone bopped in place but quick

(He can really order some colored people around . . . a sight
  to behold)
And does a basically good militant shuffle when dancing is in
  order

I'd really like to see him party more but he swears
Asphalt is bad for his eye-talian shoes
And we all appreciate eye-tal
don't we

I tried to talk to him once but he just told me
"Don't be emotional"
And all the while he was shaking and crying and raining blows
  on
poor black me

So I guess I'm wrong again
Just maybe I don't know the colour of my
truefriends
As Wilmington pointed out to me himself

But I'm still not going to anymore banquits

The last one they replaced jello with
jellied gass (a Due-pontee speciality; housewise)
And I couldn't figure out what they were trying to tell me
Wilmington said they were giving me guest treat-meants

But some how I don't feel welcome
So I'm going to pack my don-key (ass wise) and split
before they start to do me favors too

For Saundra

i wanted to write
a poem
that rhymes
but revolution doesn't lend
itself to be-bopping

then my neighbor
who thinks i hate
asked—do you ever write
tree poems—i like trees
so i thought
i'll write a beautiful green tree poem
peeked from my window
to check the image
noticed the school yard was covered
with asphalt
no green—no trees grow
in manhattan

then, well, i thought the sky
i'll do a big blue sky poem
but all the clouds have winged
low since no-Dick was elected

so i thought again
and it occurred to me
maybe i shouldn't write
at all
but clean my gun
and check my kerosene supply

perhaps these are not poetic
times
at all

My Poem

i am 25 years old
black female poet
wrote a poem asking
nigger can you kill
if they kill me
it won't stop
the revolution

i have been robbed
it looked like they knew
that i was to be hit
they took my tv
my two rings
my piece of african print
and my two guns
if they take my life
it won't stop
the revolution

my phone is tapped
my mail is opened
they've caused me to turn
on all my old friends
and all my new lovers
if i hate all black
people
and all negroes
it won't stop
the revolution

i'm afraid to tell
my roommate where i'm going
and scared to tell
people if i'm coming

if i sit here
for the rest
of my life
it won't stop
the revolution

if i never write
another poem
or short story
if i flunk out
of grad school
if my car is reclaimed
and my record player
won't play
and if i never see
a peaceful day
or do a meaningful
black thing
it won't stop
the revolution

the revolution
is in the streets
and if i stay on
the 5th floor
it will go on
if i never do
anything
it will go on

Nikki Giovanni was born in Knoxville, Tennessee, in 1943 and spent her growing up years in Cincinnati, Ohio, which she considers her home town. She studied under John Killens in the writers' workshop at Fisk University where she edited the literary magazine and helped establish the campus chapter of SNCC. In her own words, she was "kicked out of Fisk plus I dropped out of a Masters Program at the University of Pennsylvania." She has taught English at the SEEK program in New York and has been very busy giving readings at various colleges and civic centers, on radio and on television. She is now teaching at Livingston College in New Jersey.

At the age of twenty-six, Nikki Giovanni has been called "one of the most powerful figures on the new black poetry scene—both in language and appeal." This appeal has led to her being featured in *The New York Times* and in *Mademoiselle*. It is a response to the force and the gentleness that are both present in her work. "I come from a long line of fighters," she says, and when you read "My Poem" you know the line goes on. When you read her other work, you know that for her, as for all of us, the pleasures and tragedies of the individual's life and emotional self also go on.

Miss Giovanni has published two books, *Black Judgement* and *Black Feelings, Black Talk*, both done by Broadside Press. A combined edition will be published in 1970 by William Morrow and Co.

Michael S. Harper

Proposition 15

Christmas eve and no presents;
the snow's in the mountains;
the fat saint hasn't gotten
his witless teamwork from ski
trails and mushroomed mountaintops;
the lake water is truly sky-blue—
everybody's waiting for dark.
The minstrels take the lawns
to attract the skyflies
coming at midnight, in flight,
red-suited saint, with his whip
and his sack full of toys:
it can't be Halloween.

My backyard is covered with snow;
eight rabbits in reins settle their
cottontail feet in the molasses earth
and begin their whimsical dancing,
a figure-eight cycle
of rhythm and blues.

I see rose-thorned tambourines: see
that green honey-dewed fruit,
see the white sheets and pillow cases;
see that grayhaired black story-teller
on the porch swing;
even you are a believer.

Black Study

No one's been told
that black men
went first to the moon
the dark side
for dark brothers
without space ship
gravity complex
in our computer centers
government campuses
instant play and replay
white mice and pig-guineas
in concentric digital rows.

Someone has been
pulling brother's curls
into fancy barbed wire,
measuring his forelegs,
caressing his dense innards
into formaldehyde
pruning the jellied marrow:
a certain formula is appearing:
someone has been studying you.

Ode to Tenochtitlan

for Tommy Smith & John Carlos

Socks and gloves
the medal of honor
ablaze in twin fists

of two men
blackened in the imperial fires;
they stand before Coltrane
in their beauty,
the new emblem—
ANOTHER BROTHER GONE—
a style so resilient
and chromatic the pure
reeds of their bodies
bulge through metric
distances in their
special rhythms.
The impossible bowels
of round forms
digest the air
of the television
cameras in
a new vision
now on Olympus;
moon-children,
Gemini, the black stopwatch.

We have heard
the cries
bend the index,
the word-form
plumed black,
the traditional images.
Who can understand
having thought life
was somehow,
transmuted and cleansed
transistored
into a machine.

34

In the heats,
in the instant replays,
amidst the circuits
of brain waves
come back into rhythm
rhythm with a fisted
victory in another
game, a new
current, a new
exchange, a new
vision:
as a twin black spirit,
brother's come on home.

Effendi

for McCoy Tyner

The piano hums
again the clear
story of our coming,
enchained, severed,
our tongues gone,
herds the quiet
musings of ten million
years blackening the earth
with blood and our moon women,
children we loved,
the jungle swept up
in our rhapsodic song
giving back
banana leaves and

the incessant beating
of our tom-tom hearts.
We have sung a long time here
with the cross and the cotton field.
Those white faces turned
away from their mythical
beginnings are no art
but that of violence—
the kiss of death.
Somewhere on the inside
of those faces
are the real muscles
of the world;
the ones strengthened
in experience and pain,
the ones wished for in one's lover
or in the mirror
near the eyes
that record this lost, dogged data
and is pure, new, even lovely
and is you.

Where Is My Woman Now

for Billie Holiday

poplars lean backward
greener and sparser
on windward side
where is my woman now
caught in northern spit
losing the weak leaves

and winter bark
the rains till the hillside
while the poppies mope
where is my woman now
on the slopes are sparrows
bathing like sheep
in this spring muck
where is my woman now

Aftermath

Blacks all dead
in the streets;
the guerrillas run
white sympathizers in,
out of the hills;
the city streets are
brush fires of the last
lovely battle.
There were those who did
not believe, on both sides,
in the fury of those last
night's human fires;
ready-made armies
hunt even the freeways.
Now the flames suck
kerosened human flesh
as the hostages loom,
military twigs
in this medicinal barbecue:
the country, finally, is white with snow.

The Black Angel

Childhood games,
played without innocence,
and in place of the angel,
take me to a grove of pepper trees;
they lighten my head.
Trees emit their odors,
a natural oxygen tent;
have you noticed the air is heavy
in trees that shed their leaves
without hesitance,
and flow with sap,
and are closest
to the angel's skin;
the eyes, each singly
wide, smarting, unreadable
as the sap, and which
recount the games,
verses, puzzles of other men:
I am reading poems
to this black angel.
Kindled in the shrill
eloquence of other men,
the angel forces open my hands
and in the palms
leaves her footprints.

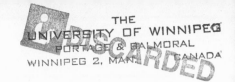
We Assume

on the death of our son, Reuben Masai Harper

We assume
that in 28 hours,
lived in a collapsible isolette,
you learned to accept pure oxygen
as the natural sky;
the scant shallow breaths
that filled those hours
cannot, did not make you fly—
but dreams were there
like crooked palmprints on
the twin-thick windows of the nursery—
in the glands of your mother.

We assume
the sterile hands
drank chemicals in and out
from lungs opaque with mucus,
pumped your stomach,
eeked the bicarbonate in
crooked, green-winged veins,
out in a plastic mask;

A woman who'd lost her first son
consoled us with an angel gone ahead
to pray for our family—
gone into that sky
seeking oxygen,
gone into autopsy,
a fine brown powdered sugar,
a disposable cremation:

We assume
you did not know we loved you.

Another Season

for Shirl

She tells me she feels
flutters for the fourth time
in three years.

Rain and wind scuff
four inches of leaves
to a porch full of toys—

our first son's—
another and another
season come on

and a child climbs
up her womb
towards her belly.

I've written poems
intentionally
to wash off

Reuben, Michael;
Reuben, Michael,
gone on.

Now I write this poem,
early, feeling the movement
in the belly go on.

New Season

for Shirl

My woman has picked
all the leaves,
rolled her hands into locks,
gone into the woods
where I have taught her
the language of these wood leaves,
and the red sand plum trees.
It is a digest
of my taking these leaves with hunger;
it is love she understands.
From my own wooden smell
she has shed her raisin skin
and come back
sweetened into brilliant music:
Her song is our new season.

MICHAEL S. HARPER: "Born, March 18, 1938, in Brooklyn, New York; moved with family to Los Angeles in 1951; B.A., M.A., in English, Cal State, Los Angeles; M.A. in English (creative writing emphasis), U of Iowa; taught at Los Angeles City College, Contra Costa College in San Pablo, California, Reed, and Lewis and Clark (poet-in-residence), Cal State, Hayward (currently, Associate Professor of English); fellowship, Center for Advanced Study, U of Illinois, Urbana, Illinois, 70–71; married, two sons.

"Poems have appeared in: *Burning Deck, Carolina Quarterly, December, Midwestern University Quarterly, Poetry Northwest, Quarterly Review of Literature, Southern Review, Sunday Oregonian* (Portland), *Negro Digest, Poetry.* A collection of poems, *Dear John, Dear Coltrane,* published by the University of Pittsburgh Press, will appear in 1970; a second collection, *History Is Your Own Heartbeat,* is now in manuscript."

"My first book of poems, *Dear John, Dear Coltrane,* took me ten years to write; that is, the poems stretch over a ten-year period and suggest an orientation, a focus, a point of view I think is special. John Coltrane was the epitome of a new style, his music and being the vision of liberation, the total liberation of the sensibility expressed through the man and his art, the tenor and soprano saxophones the vehicles for the larger man, a force so overwhelming as to be revolutionary to perception and sensibility themselves. My vision has been slow in coming to the surface. What concerns me is the articulation of *consciousness,* the ability to deal with contingencies and create a new liberating vision which frees rather than imprisons.

"Some of the themes of my poems are: History and the development of an historical consciousness which frees us from the past; *modes* of perception, the relationship between ideal, real, and material modes of individual perception; myths, distinctions between truth and lie, the one the patterning of particular experiences into universals, the other the incapacity to accept facts as particular because of the demands of a system (one of which is the closed system of white supremacy, one dimensional, cyclic, repetitious in design and in error); personality, the deepening of historical consciousness to facilitate an awakening, psychic and real.

"My poems are *modal*. By modality I mean the creation of an environment so intense by its life and force as to revivify and regenerate, spiritually, man and community; modality assumes contact, touch, between human beings, one to one, and an environment of spirit that revitalizes man, individually and culturally. Man is the original *mode;* what he does is modal—the musicians, Bud, Bird, Trane, Lady, Bessie, Pres, Fats, Mingus Elvin, Max, McCoy, Miles, were and are modal; man's being, his sensibility in action, contact, with another human being, is modality. The blues singer says 'I' but the audience assumes 'We'; out of such energy comes community and freedom. A Love Supreme!"

William J. Harris

My Friend, Wendell Berry

My friend, Wendell Berry
bought a pocket watch
like this one:

for 25¢
off the back of a truck in San Francisco.
He was real excited and happy
about his shrewd deal.
I, a sophisticated midwesterner
with an $80
watch
like this one

given to me by my mother
was simply unimpressed
and a little amused.
You see, Wendell is from
a couple of miles
below the Ohio River

and I'm from several
miles above the Ohio River
in the lap of culture.

Well, yesterday, my $80 watch
broke
and Wendell offered
to sell me his watch
for 50¢
—that would be a 100% profit!
So I went to
this discount place, Baz'r
and bought a watch
like this one:

for $3.66. Obviously a better watch
than Wendell's.
But I ain't never
talking to Mr. Wendell Berry again.

With My Napalm Six Shooters

Here
     I go
with my napalm
             six shooters.

First I incinerate
furry King Kong
before he can grab
         Fay Wray

45

that white American beauty,
hanging from Empire State Buildings
     and Washington Monuments.

(Oh, yellow flaming monkey.)

We must protect
our women
from the wild beasts
of the world.

(A lady from Columbus, Ohio
writes:
Please, Mr. Harris,
no vivid
   images.
I have a weak stomach.)

Sorry, lady.
From henceforth
THIS SHALL BE A LOVE POEM.

I look tenderly
    at my girl's
boyish
  face
—she's beautiful even
though
    she has big teeth.
Then I put
    my napalm
six shooter
in her down-turned
     mouth
and she says
    yes and roses
as I pull the trigger.

46

We Live in a Cage

We live in a cage.
We demand drapes.
It is a matter of our dignity.

They say they don't have any
and anyway they are not allowed.
Privacy is obsolete.

We say all right but we have the right
to answer the phone
nude. We pay our bills.

They say when we answer
the phone, we must
wear robes no shorter than 2 inches

above the knee.
It is simply
a matter of decency.

We say all right but we have the right
to make love
without the aid of the neighbors.

They say we have no rights
and threaten to take our cage
away from us.

I, Satan

I, Satan, the Prince of Hell,
have become hopelessly outmoded
even in Catholic boys' dreams.
In the face of modern, efficient
and man-made evil
I look hopelessly quaint
like a small town buffoon,
perhaps a little drunk,
dressed in an ancient costume,
challenging
an army of tanks and flame throwers
with a wooden pitchfork.

For Bill Hawkins, a Black Militant

Night, I know you are powerful and artistic
                in your misspellings.
How distinctively I sense your brooding,
feel your warm breath against my face,
hear your laughter—not cruel only amused
                and arrogant: young—
insisting on my guilt.
Night, let me be part of you
                but in my own dark way.

48

Samantha Is My Negro Cat

Samantha is my
Negro cat.
Black with yellow eyes.
A big flat nose.
Thick features.
She came to me
from the street.
(A street nigger
with hairless ears.)
She's tough.
Been a mother too.
Has hard pink nipples.
(Yes, pink. She also has
a white spot on her neck.
She ain't pure. But
I don't care. I ain't no racist.)
She has a sad high ass.
Sway-back.
Not much to look at
but as affectionate
as any girl who's
had a hard time of it.
"Bums," said the vet
a little too objectively,
"always respond to love."

Samantha rubs against
me, sits across my
lap, purring her short-circuited purr.

Lady, this man is
going to treat you better
than the rest.

(You say you've heard that one before.)
We'll comfort each other
in the evenings
after supper, when we stare
out on the
cold and dark street.

Habitual

Sometimes, the octopus wraps
his arms around my neck,
sucking vigorously
with his chalk red tentacles.
                    He grows numb,
stops, winks, and confides to me
he is my buddy—a real friend.

Other times, while I stroll the deck,
he sneaks up behind me
and squirts black India ink
on my white Captain's uniform.

And other times, when the octopus
isn't around, there is the whale
who hovers near the ship.
He has the eyes of a dead man
—unmoving but accusing.
He asks, a hurt look on his face,
"What's wrong with you?
Why are you so nervous?
Where is your confidence?"
Usually I quietly tiptoe away.

A Winter Song

If I
were the
cold weather
and people
talked about me
the way they talk
about it,
I'd just
pack up
and leave town.

Can I Write You an Anthem

Can I write you an anthem
Yellow Springs, Ohio?

It is time for love
of my woman and the small town
where I walked with Bill Cook
down the middle of Xenia
Avenue to be the first
to walk in the new snow
—with Chief McKee
telling us
you can't walk down the middle
of the main street
—even Yellow Springs has laws
—then asking us where we
were going
and taking us there.

But it is not time
for love of you, America.
I have never slept with you
or even bitched about the holes
in your streets.

America, you are something
strange and dark
down below Goes*

---

* Goes—an even smaller town than Yellow Springs, a couple of miles
south of Y.S.O. on U.S. 68.

WILLIAM J. HARRIS

"WILLIAM J. HARRIS was born on March 12, 1942, in Yellow Springs, Ohio. He graduated from Central State University in 1968 and was a M.A. candidate in Creative Writing at Stanford University during the year 1968–69. He is presently in the Ph.D. program in English at Stanford. He has published in *The Antioch Review, The Beloit Poetry Journal, Intro, Nine Black Poets,* and others. He will have poems in *Black Out Loud* and *Galaxy of Black Writing* later this year."

"A fat, unpleasant professor of mine once said: 'You write poems because you want to be loved.' Maybe. A lot of my poetry is love letters—poems reaching out to touch someone else. Especially when that someone else is forbidden. Yet I write for other—and I think better—reasons. I try to understand the world around me. To my mind, a poem is a concentrated, concrete, and living meditation on the nature of practically everything and everyone. Mainly, everyone. One of the most successful meditations I ever encountered was Satyajit Ray's *The Apu Trilogy.* He does in film what I want to do in verse: he says, shows (making us feel and understand on the most elemental level) what it means to be a man—a man in the world."

David Henderson

Poem for Painters

to Joe Overstreet

the tree tries to grow thru the window
of joe's loft high on bowery
thats my tree/ say joe
we take care of each other
it grows with me
the tree

in summer twilight
the green leaves shimmer
vibrates the news
of whats to come
of what has gone.
you see it next to the tv
floating eternally
a simple message
adjunct a complex machine

men rush against each other
in the karmic sport of fear/
the poor people in D.C.
at their insurrection city
take mud baths
they wallow like african animals.

DAVID HENDERSON

programs flash hour to hour
a flick of the wrist alters
the channel of the image/
                    outside
              the leaves of the tree
        ripples ancient news of an eternal thing
      symbols signs psyches/ painters of the trees

calls
in the news
of what is to come
brings the painters of pluck and sport
from far off lands
cross the brooklyn bridge
from wall street
from city hall
and lower east side
air lofts of manhattan island
                    white and jaxon
                    osby and whitten
                    waters and the ancient rivers
              freelance
                    charters of the universe

the leaves of the breeze
ripple in the trees
the leaves in the paintings
upon the off white walls
call down flying arrows
black people dancing
round a burning block
from a far off view
a man
in the embrace
of a tree/

once
a mad scientist
built a television
into the trunk
of a tree
the
     tree grew electric leaves
scantified
by the nation

the screen glows blue grey smoke
The Poor People on the march again
forty acres of black folks
& a mule
drawing their leader
in a long box

the leaves of the trees
brings the news of far off lands

a look out the window
thru the trees of joes loft
see the winos and the workers
see the traffic and debris
see the time etched on a famous structure of the street

in jaxon's temple
an entire structure above bowery
we walk the long floors
joe/ jaxon painters paint words
against the ceiling/ against the wall
joe say/

                    i like to see in a work of art
                    a man trying to push a boulder
                              up a steel hill

we drain the pluck
ignite the mojo

56

watch the west horizon above the stores
watch the east horizon above the parking lot
the day sings   flies
high above boweryroofs
joe say/

                when you ask me what i like
                i like the problems i'm involved in
                        that's what i like

jaxon from chicago town
middle western blues singer
by transmission of the dance

                joe say/what i want to get
                    out of your work
                    is something to help me
                    with mine

along the long walls
a colonial loft of original city
the stain of ages in brick
the rafters and roof beams
speak the symbols of age
of time worn thin
abramelin the mage
within

i write in the traffic
in the thick of it
or in the hollow of a lonely cafe
where white men come to eat white food
                of the institutional state
i write in the debris
            of traffic trends

on a corner of the block
where the sun goes upside my head

at the famous
Bowery Follies nursinghome night club
drone tourist buses disgorge cargoes
into the bowery's historical landmark
for the fat lady and the dwarf
for rudy vallee's orchestra
daily revival
speak camp
etched in the color of cartoons
etched in the soundwaves of time

i write in traffic
cross the street
a man lay dead
for all intent.
the sun lolls on the rooftops
the oriental children
are trying to shine shoes
hawking in the street
the way of tao
times is getting hard.

call to the windows
under the tree
hey joe!
whatcha doing with that gun
in your hand?
           when the shit go down
          i got ten bullets/ thats all

i own this house
this is *my* tree

architect of the beyond
in a doom domed city
the bowery
is adjacent wall street
for all intents
and all purposes.
walk thru the blocks
the only exercise
we get/

       we come to the door under the limbs
       joe say/

> *get out of my doorstep, man. you cant sleep*
> *here. look. you pissed all over yourself. get up*
> *man. take your wine. you got some left. david,*
> *you got your blade? looks like we gonna have*
> *to cut this motherfucker. get up man. we*
> *gonna cut you. thats the only way to get him*
> *up. get up man!*

those
who are often called men
stained by their own dung
(you could call it ecology)
urine crotched and barefoot
wine sweetened black eyes
staggering
in the nursing home of the welfare state
flop housed and abandoned
death in the street for the brave
inmates of the aged the lost pigeons
flock
to the spray of bread

as those on bowery
flock
for the sale
of cut-rate wine
made from the labor
of those who cut and die
just the same
workers of constant migration
from field to field
ratio of the tour
of duty/
        the poor people
march across the TV screen
led by an irate irish priest
they demonstrate in miami
where they are shot
by burns detectives
for going near the ocean

the leaves of the trees
mourn the news of the land

i write in the mindflow of traffic
macktrucks explode the fume of daze
in the luncheonette of delancy street
adjacent the toils of the Catholic Workers

the truck drivers partake . . .
the horse fly fan blows the street to a draw
cigarettes are sold
thru a slot in the window

witness the picture of mass metal fatigue
dropping metal scrap blood on the tar-plane lanes

we walk the space of joe's loft
the child runs in the plane
reflects his parents

reflects the tree
the old man of the space
disperses the action of jobs
by forceful gestures
weaponless combat
of the arm the hand the stare
timbre of the voice set of the lip
dance a dance
charted long ago
in memphis

the nest spins ancient tribal hut
images evolve the off white walls
the tree whirls outside
it comes thru the window
sits down for supper
a wheel in a wheel of fortune
showering silver leaves
say/ stick with me baby
you got nothing to lose.

the paintings of the trees
tell the news
of the days

distant travelers converge at the narrow door
the ripples of the leaves form an arch
and hail to the boys
huffing and puffing
jaxon sonny and osby
pursued by a nation of puerto ricans
from the lower east side
over roofs fireescapes
thru sewers under parked cars
over moving cars
from avenue "B"
thru the park

chased by flailing sticks
the patter of sixty feets
a symphony of congas
stomping wind
amok on the lower east side

thru the leaves of the laughing trees
comes the news of the land

the leo sun beams at the street
human mucous membrane pools on urban sidewalks
heavy decibel trucks
bomb
concrete and tar
shadow storms of high vapor gas
blow all over the planet/
     aims for the moon

    o how it tickles to see insanity flow
    ask the hollow men/ they ought to know

in the room
above the tree
above the street
mad painters and practical wives
assemble apple pie
the children run across the hut floor
tribal and eternal
on the screen
the poor people land in Paris/
confetti and bouquets
drift thru the air
as the French national anthem is played

we recall
the best minds in the streets
frail and pale

62

DAVID HENDERSON

with the white powder of the white rooms
haranguing and shit
as kaufman told allan the g. once
a passage of words
transmission of time/

the traffic flows
the tree stands
like
a natural man

DAVID HENDERSON was born in Harlem in 1942, one of the three Manhattan-born poets in this anthology, and he went to two New York colleges, Hunter and the New School for Social Research. His first book, *Felix of the Silent Forest*, appeared in 1967. His work has been published widely in magazines and in anthologies. E. P. Dutton is bringing out his latest collection of poetry, *De Mayor of Harlem*, in 1970.

Mr. Henderson has been involved a good deal with young writers. During the 1968–69 school year, he worked with the Teachers and Writers Collaborative at I.S. 55 in Ocean Hill. He has been a member of the Collaborative's Board of Directors.

Audre Lorde

Naturally

Since Naturally Black is Naturally Beautiful
I must be proud
And, naturally,
Black and
Beautiful
Who always was a trifle
Yellow
And plain though proud
Before.

I've given up pomades
Having spent the summer sunning
And feeling naturally free
    (if I die of skin cancer
    oh well—one less
    black and beautiful me)
Yet no Agency spends millions
To prevent my summer tanning
And who trembles nightly
With the fear of their lily cities being swallowed
By a summer ocean of naturally woolly hair?

But I've bought my can of
Natural Hair Spray
Made and marketed in Watts
Still thinking more
Proud beautiful black women
Could better make and use
Black bread.

Fantasy and Conversation

Speckled frogs leap from my mouth
To drown in the coffee
Between our wisdoms
And decision.

I could smile
And turn these frogs into white pearls
Speak of love, our making and giving.
And if the spell works
Will I break down
Or build what is broken
Into a new house
Shook with confusion
Will I strike
Before our magic
Turns colour?

The Woman Thing

The hunters are back
From beating the winter's face
In search of a challenge or task
In search of food
Making fresh tracks for their children's hunger
They do not watch the sun
They cannot wear its heat for a sign
Of triumph or freedom
The hunters are treading heavily homeward
Through snow that is marked
With their own footprints
Emptyhanded the hunters return
Snow-maddened, sustained by their rages.

In the night, after food
They will seek
Young girls for their amusement.
Now the hunters are coming
And the unbaked girls flee from their angers.
All this day I have craved
Food for my child's hunger.
Emptyhanded the hunters come shouting
Injustices drip from their mouths
Like stale snow melted in sunlight.

And this womanthing my mother taught me
Bakes off its covering of snow
Like a rising blackening sun.

7/2

Perhaps it was the bleak street
On Sunday afternoon searching for a leftover paper
That finally convinced me
Austerity was for the bird's time only
Singing the East Seventh Blues
September and another winter upon me
That made me enter your body house
Looking for warmth, a blood charge
I could store up against December
Con Edison not paid and persistent
Even radiant heaters proving untrue.

Or am I lying after the fact
Sated with pride and the sound
Of my door slamming behind you
As a new cold comes seeping in?

And What about the Children

Now we've made a child
And the dire predictions
Have changed to wild
Grim
Speculations.
Still
The negatives are waiting
Watching
And the relatives
Keep Right On Touching . . .

AUDRE LORDE

(and how much curl
is right for a girl?)

If it is said—
At some future date—
That my son's head
Is on straight
He won't care
About his hair

Nor give a damn
Whose wife I am.

Rites of Passage

to MLK jr.

Now rock the boat to a fare-thee-well.
Once we suffered dreaming
Into the place where the children are playing
Their child's games
Where the children are hoping
Knowledge survives if
Unknowing
They follow the game
Without winning.

Their fathers are dying
Back to the freedom
Of wise children playing
At knowing
Their fathers are dying
Whose deaths will not free them

Of growing from knowledge
Of knowing
When the game becomes foolish
A dangerous pleading
For time out of power.

Quick
Children kiss us
We are growing through dream.

Bloodbirth

That which is inside of me screaming
Beating about for exit or entry
Names the wind, wanting wind's voice
Wanting wind's power
It is not my heart
I am trying to tell this
Without art or embellishment
With bits of me flying out in all directions
Screams memories old pieces of flesh
Struck off like dry bark
From a felled tree, bearing
Up or out
Holding or bringing forth
Child or demon
Is this birth or exorcism
Or the beginning machinery of myself
Outlining recalling
My father's business—what I must be
About, my own business
Minding.

Shall I split
Or be cut down by a word's complexion
Or the lack of it
And from what direction
Will the opening be made
To show the true faces of me
Lying exposed and together
My children your children their children
Bent on our conjugating business.

The American Cancer Society or There Is More Than One Way to Skin a Coon

Of all the ways in which this country
Prints its death upon me
Selling me cigarettes is one of the least certain.
Every day I watch my son digging
ConEdison GeneralMotors GarbageDisposal
Out of his nose as he watches the 3 second spot
Called How To Stop Smoking
And it makes me sick to my stomach.
For it is not by cigarettes
That you intend to destroy my children.

Not even by the cold white light of moon-walks
While half the boys I knew
Are doomed to quicker trips by a different capsule;
No, the american society destroys
By seductive and reluctant admissions
For instance

Black women no longer give birth through their ears
And therefore must have A Monthly Need For Iron Pills:
For instance
Our Pearly teeth are *not* racially insured
And therefore must be Gleemed For Fewer Cavities:
For instance
Even though all astronauts are white
Perhaps Black People *can* develop
Some human attributes
Requiring
Dried dog food frozen coffee instant oatmeal
Depilatories deodorants detergents
And other assorted plastic.

And this is the surest sign I know
That the american cancer society is dying—
It has started to dump its symbols onto Black People
A convincing proof
Those symbols are now useless
And far more lethal than emphysema.

A Poem for a Poet

I always think of a coffin's quiet
When I sit in the world of my car
Observing
Particularly when the windows are closed and washed clean
By the rain. I like to sit there sometimes
And watch other worlds pass. Yesterday evening
Waiting Jennie, another chapter,
I sat in my car on Sheridan Square

Flat and broke and a little bit damp
Thinking about money and rain and how
The Village broads with their narrow hips
Rolled like drunken shovels down Christopher Street.

Then I saw you unmistakably
Darting out between a police car
And what used to be Atkins' all-night diner
On the corner of Fourth and Sheridan Square
Where we sat making bets the last time I saw you
On how many busts we could count through the plateglass
    windows
In those last skinny hours before dawn
With our light worded out but still burning
And the evening's promise dregs in our coffee cups—
And I saw you dash out and turn left at the corner
Your beard spiky with rain and refusing
Shelter under your chin.

I had thought you were dead Jarrell
Struck down by a car at sunset on a North Carolina Road
Or maybe you were the driver
Tricked into a fatal swerve by some twilit shadow
Or was that Frank O'Hara
Or Conrad Kent Rivers
And you were the lonesome spook in a Windy City motel
Draped in the secrets of your convulsive death
All alone
All poets all loved and dying alone
That final death less real than those deaths you lived
And for which I forgave you.

I watched you hurry down Fourth Street Jarrell
From the world of my car in the rain
Remembering Spring Festival night
At Women's College in North Carolina and
Wasn't that world a coffin

Retreat of spring whispers romance and rhetoric
Untouched by the winds buffeting up the road from Greenville
And nobody mentioned the Black Revolution or Sit-Ins
Or Freedom Rides or SNCC or cattle-prods in Jackson,
    Mississippi—
Where I was to find myself how many years later;
/You were mistaken that night and I told you so
In the letter that began—Dear Jarrell,
If you sit in one place long enough
The whole world will pass you by. . . .
You were wrong that night when you said
I took my living too seriously
Meaning—you were afraid I might take you too seriously,
And you shouldn't have worried, because
Although I always dug you too much to put you down
I never took you at all
Except as a good piece of my first journey South,
Except as I take you now gladly and separate
At a distance and wondering
As I have so often, how come
Being so cool, you weren't also a little bit
Black.

And also why you have returned to this dying city
And what piece of me is it then
Buried down in North Carolina.

AUDRE LORDE is one of the rare New York writers who can call the city her birthplace. Born in Manhattan in 1934, she went to Hunter College and then to Columbia University, where she received her master's degree. After this she spent a year at the University of Mexico. She says of herself:

"I am Black, Woman, and Poet;—fact, and outside the realm of choice. I can choose only to be or not be, and in various combinations of myself. And as my breath is a part of my breathing, my eyes of my seeing, all that I am is of who I am, is of what I do. The shortest statement of philosophy I have is my living, or the word 'I.'

"Having made homes in most parts of this city, I hang now from the west edge of Manhattan, and at any moment I can cease being a New Yorker, for already my children betray me in television, in plastic, in misplaced angers.

"In 1968, under a National Endowment to the Arts Grant, I spent some time as Poet in Residence at Tougaloo College in Jackson, Mississippi, where I became convinced, anti-academic though I am, that poets must teach what they know if we are to continue being.

"At the City University of New York, I teach young people."

75

L. V. Mack

Mad Man's Blues

". . . even if your head was cut off,
or each finger
twisted
from its shape until it broke,
and you screamed too
with the other, in pleasure."
    —ROBERT CREELEY

These good many mornings have I risen,
with blood on my hands and, thought it was the earth's
and was mine.
& after the daylight wished for the morning,
again, to go down to the shore with the old men
who shake their fists and shout
at the tumbling clouds,
or the water
              and the white spray,
or the wind itself
gobbles their speech.

Over a Glass of Wine

"wouldn't you agree the best curve
she has now think. how you've run your hand on
the back of her thigh,
& over her buttock . . ."
                              the other nodded
& his eyes grew large he
took a scissors and snipped
off the man's head

Biafra

Biafra should be the name of a woman,
black and soft. smooth
belly,
and a heavy breast.

Biafra.
listen to the way she walks.

Biafra.
listen to the way she walks.

the black little boy
dozes in the hot sun.
Biafra.
she brings the burn of day.

Biafra. O mother, hear the growl, the night
is cold, cold, cold.

i am sleepy
when will she find me
where will i find you
where will i find you

Zeus in August

we'll mambo thru the thickest
nights   you
many bellied from children
you pained for

I stick to your wet breasts
drink your wet thighs

Piece

*"like any lost lover I cannot believe the loss
of love   you!   you!   you!"*
—MAX FINSTEIN

then there is no more,
and love has taken its
incredible way
out the door. our bodies
have come back to themselves
to stand there waiting for
something.

78

Death Songs

1. White As I See It Rising

for L.V.

it is midnite. the room is blue.
the night is a blank
like a white clock face, something
i will not remember.

i have forgotten
you,
and the blue night,
     and the morning colors: red,
white
as i see it rising
until it has blinded me
in the eyes,
               a needle of light in
     the center. of my head.
i have forgotten.
i have forgotten you.

2. The Eye Fills Itself with Light

the fragile night—a look of death might
turn it like flowers as light as snow:
through the hole
is a sleep of light, a fine dust in nothing.
sprinkle the light into the black;
in the crossing of the void,
shatter the night with fear.

3. The Eye Is a Hole in Light

do not look for me
in the night
the flowers have the look of death.
                              the eye
is a hole in light, & the night is a mirror

that the warmth of fright turns to water
chasing into nothing.

4. What Little You Know

what little you know
is not enough to live. you know everything.
you know
that you know nothing, can be sure of
nothing.
even the apparition
                    of white death
is something you do not know, that
you will forget at the instant of light (when
do you become dead?) you
never knew.
you relinquish your lover, the soft flesh,
your children, you no longer
are waiting, there is nothing
                              for you.

5. A Flower Has a Light of Its Own

but the light—
                    if you shut all the doors
there is still the light. and when the room is a black
you will still see the flowers and to shut them in
to close all the light in &
step into the night,
naked, except for the look
of fear

when the night is a flower
of white light that
the look
could turn into nothing.

you do not see the night, blinded
by the memory of everything

that you have forgotten   that
you will forget.

Jungle Fever

in some time becoming
with-less-strength

i remember the anger the
ta(a)r in the heart.
(the dull-eyed. Moon-girl.
under the heavy blows.)

in some time
becoming with
less strength,
—she has become pale
and mindless
& i am breathless & half-dead.

In some false time
We are gnawing on Love's bones—
remnants where
ever she kneels
& rises.
What is She
that She separates me bone
by bone . . . ? *Mercy*
Mercy
: the fierce touch put upon us.

L. V. MACK: "I am twenty-three now, started writing at eighteen. (Incidentally, born B'klyn, N.Y., May 6, 1947; attended school at Tenn. A & I for a while; recently have been to Mexico and the West Coast. Everything's just happenin'.)"

"A poem is an organism of soul consciousness. At my better moments I have no use for language. Hopefully when I speak, it is divine; they will listen and later, I will listen to what they heard."

Clarence Major

In Chapala, Jal

during a night in a red mud
    colored 30 pesos per day hotel room
                    we sat yoga late
        into the uncomfortable
           hours bed
reading lines & railroads after the disaster
        of Tizapan
      just a slow disappointment
            coming into the corners of our unpaved
senses the worst dark room
                in your skull when the
      lights are damp unforgiving reflections
            nobody shows anybody such a room
sick looking dogs drag themselves
      along the filthy streets of Tizapan no
  tourist anywhere
            everywhere the horror of so many
                  Texas license plates
I want to blow this town baby,
            in the morning we go back
    to Guadalajara

Is Natural, Takes Me In

```
            my sense
of my       self a
     black self
unshocking to
Mexican eyes the
                  innermost coat
of the form, the       perception
            is gentle
            is
natural, takes me in
            so
                  beautifully so
sensibly
```

Guadalajara

```
            we shall go on to
        the other side
of the lake, even
                  suspect we shall return       Tho I
      dread it(wrongly
                        from ignorance
    to Guadalajara
a beautiful city not hasty not
                  the place I thot it was.Break-
fast under a polkadot canopy yet here
                        just as many
      Arkansas & Texas eyes
                  as in that shitty town Chapala
```

The dead skin of their boneskull
                    cracks as they perceive
            us Africa & Europe in the
                    Mexican rain married without
                    raincoats
                            after 6 splendid weeks
                            by the ocean, a little dusty from
the roads but
                    in love holding hands, the ocean every moment
still in my sanity

Weak Dynamite

                            he was fretful
it happened again it was forced this
time
                    as far as
he could go
                    !broke out: a   BLOOD STORM
beneath his palms his
                            feet imagine a
woman living with "it"
                    : It was embarrassing for him, too
ItellYou

                            nor did he intend to
touch another he
was sure the   assurance was his
            TOMORROW

                            anyway he had discovered a
                    secret

he could laugh
talk
and almost make sense but his
arrogance
was a defensive way by which
SOUNDS
drop-
ped
all through his   woman and his
tongue
got disconnected from the flesh of his
words
HE MEANT NOT TO KNOCK HER OUT WITH
BUT ONLY TO
DISINFECT HER WITH

always a fretful man with
a
doctor's record easily his
biography
(no painful and beautiful development
to look back on)

the weak dynamite of his
"manhood"
hung
(SHOCKED IN
AN END-
less laugh)
by his fumbled definition of it
between them.

it happened again
and again
WITHOUT RITUAL

Pictures

Negro girls
like 12 years old, in
   [enclaves]
midwest ENDS
   in integrated
LIQUID SLANG BRANCHES OF TERMINAL BRICKS
that is, integrated in-
to   the red bricks of these
     years,

behind TVvoices animating clumsy
     THE CLUE TO MY JUDGEment
report of BLACK respiration
     confuse their soft
solid simplicity, & they carry white
     wallets, they do not
carry pictures of *light* in these
     their INTEGRATED heaviness
coming clearly back to a simple/sound
     MOTIVE for
carrying snapshots of friends
     fallout beautiful if they now
see the lineage loveliness of THEMSELVES
     & schoolmates as any face

Dynamite Transported
from Canada to New York City

radio said FBI uncovered
plot to
   BOOM BOOM BOOM
Lady Lib
Wash Monu
Lib Bell
      I was sitting in the midwest

3 years later, the hard hand-
some turn of his chin
      2 eyes, black and steady
—this was the serious
saboteur? (working in a youthcenter
               in NYC, I am
in a sense reality.
     Now, somebody wanted to do
a book
     of his life. Was 1 of them, out
of prison? I read the tender
     intelligent poems from jail to
his mother
             in NYC I pull
the trans-
ported ends of my sense of reality &
            those radio waves
together

How to Describe Fall from Now On

(in Bourbon, consumption: a lack of beer
sets in) racklingly brown, tan unyielding leaves
    FALL FALL FALL
    FALL FALL FALL
nowhere:
    in this restless city:some sky might
fall away, warm shot with ghosts/ illusions

dots

stab the eyeballs: puzzle the acute presence
    of somany
    FALLING FALLING
down nobodys
    FALLING FALLING
downdrunk.

Winter, a cross. Calcify city
    calcify these painful alco
(not products
    but HOLICS. Figures are available

CLARENCE MAJOR was born in Atlanta, Georgia, in 1936 and grew up in Chicago, where he studied at the Art Center. A most prolific and active writer, his credits range from writing a novel, *All-Night Visitors*, and a great many stories, essays, and poems that have been printed in the United States and at least eight other countries, to editing an anthology, *New Black Poetry*. He has also been a teacher and research analyst and has given many readings and lectures.

Wesleyan University Press is publishing a book of Major's poetry, *Swallow the Lake*, in 1970. Another volume of poetry will be published by Corinth Books, and a second novel, *NO*, will be published by Emerson/Hall.

A MAJOR STATEMENT ON POETICS
"To understand its religious nature think about nothing or anything. Right On!"

N. H. Pritchard

```
            TTTTTTTTTTTT
            TTTTTTTTTTTT
                TT
                TT
                TT
                TT
                TT
        HH      TT      HH
        HH      TT      HH
        HH      TT      HH
        HH      TT      HH
        HH      TT      HH
        HH              HH
        HHHHHHHHHHHHH
        HHHHHHHHHHHHH
        HH              HH
    EE  HH              HH  EE
    EE  HH              HH  EE
    EE  HH      EE      HH  EE
    EE  HH      EE      HH  EE
    EE  HH      EE      HH  EE
    EE          EE          EE
    EEEEEEEEEEEEEEEEEEEEE
    EEEEEEEEEEEEEEEEEEEEE
```

```
                              bBb
                              bBb
                              bBb
                              bBb
                              bBb
                              bBb
                              bBb
                              bBb
                              bBb
                              bBb
                              bBb
                              bBb
                              bBb
                              bBb
                              bBb
                              bBb
                              bBb
                              bBb
                              bBb
                              bBb
bbbbbbbbbbbbbbbbbbbbbbbbbbbbbbBbbbbbbbbbbbbbbbbbbbbbbbbbbb
                               B
                               B
                               B
                               B
                               B
                               B
                               B
                               B
                               B
                               B
                               B
                               B
                               B
                               B
                               B
                               B
                               B
                               B
                               B
```

,

```
XXXXXXXXXXXXXXXXXXXXXXXXXXXXXXXXXXXX
XXXXXXXXXXXXXXXXXXXXXXXXXXXXXXXXXXXX
XXXXXXXXXXXXXXXXXXXXXXXXXXXXXXXXXXXX
XXXXXXXXXXXXXXXXXXXXXXXXXXXXXXXXXXXX
XXXXXXXXX                   XXXXXXXXX
XXXXXXXXX                   XXXXXXXXX
XXXXXXXXX                   XXXXXXXXX
XXXXXXXXX                   XXXXXXXXX
XXXXXXXXX                   XXXXXXXXX
```

```
XXXXXXXXX                   XXXXXXXXX
XXXXXXXXX                   XXXXXXXXX
XXXXXXXXX                   XXXXXXXXX
XXXXXXXXX                   XXXXXXXXX
XXXXXXXXX                   XXXXXXXXX
XXXXXXXXXXXXXXXXXXXXXXXXXXXXXXXXXXXX
XXXXXXXXXXXXXXXXXXXXXXXXXXXXXXXXXXXX
XXXXXXXXXXXXXXXXXXXXXXXXXXXXXXXXXXXX
XXXXXXXXXXXXXXXXXXXXXXXXXXXXXXXXXXXX
```

No.

aaaaaaaaaaaaaaaaaaaaaaaaaaaaaaaaaaaaa
aaaaaaaaaaaaaaaaaaaaaaaaaaaaaaaaaaaaa
aaaaaaaaaaaaaaaaaaaaaaaaaaaaaaaaaaaaa
aaaaaaaaaaaaaaaaaaaaaaaaaaaaaaaaaaaaa
        aaaaaa
        aaaaaa
        aaaaaa
        aaaaaa
        aaaaaa
        aaaaaa
        aaaaaa
        aaaaaa
        aaaaaa
        aaaaaa
        aaaaaa
        aaaaaa
        aaaaaa
        aaaaaa
        aaaaaa
        aaaaaa
        aaaaaa
        aaaaaa
        aaaaaa
        aaaaaa
        aaaaaa
aaaaaaaaaaaaaaaaaaaaaaaaaaaaaaaaaaaaa
aaaaaaaaaaaaaaaaaaaaaaaaaaaaaaaaaaaaa
aaaaaaaaaaaaaaaaaaaaaaaaaaaaaaaaaaaaa
aaaaaaaaaaaaaaaaaaaaaaaaaaaaaaaaaaaaa

```
          TTTTTTTT
          TTTTTTTT
          TTTTTTTT
          TTTTTTTT
          TTTTTTTT
          TTTTTTTT
          TTTTTTTT
          TTTTTTTT
          TTTTTTTT
          TTTTTTTT
          TTTTTTTT
          TTTTTTTT
          TTTTTTTT
          TTTTTTTT
          TTTTTTTT
          TTTTTTTT
          TTTTTTTT
TTTTTTTTTTTTTTTTTTTTTTTTTTTTT
TTTTTTTTTTTTTTTTTTTTTTTTTTTTT
TTTTTTTTTTTTTTTTTTTTTTTTTTTTT

          IIIIIIII
          IIIIIIII
          IIIIIIII
          IIIIIIII
          IIIIIIII
          IIIIIIII
          IIIIIIII
          IIIIIIII
          IIIIIIII
          IIIIIIII
          IIIIIIII
          IIIIIIII
          IIIIIIII
          IIIIIIII
          IIIIIIII
          IIIIIIII
          IIIIIIII
```

VVVV

VVVVVVVVVVVVVVVV   VVVVVVVVVVVVVVVV
VVVVVVVVVVVVVVVV   VVVVVVVVVVVVVVVV
VVVVVVVVVVVVVVVV   VVVVVVVVVVVVVVVV
VVVVVVVVVVVVVVVV   VVVVVVVVVVVVVVVV
VVVVVVVVVVVVVVVV   VVVVVVVVVVVVVVVV
VVVVVVVVVVVVVVVV   VVVVVVVVVVVVVVVV

VVVVVVVVVVVVVVVVVVVVVVVVVVVVVVVVVVVVVVVVV
VVVVVVVVVVVVVVVVVVVVVVVVVVVVVVVVVVVVVVVVV
VVVVVVVVVVVVVVVVVVVVVVVVVVVVVVVVVVVVVVVVV
VVVVVVVVVVVVVVVVVVVVVVVVVVVVVVVVVVVVVVVVV
VVVVVVVVVVVVVVVVVVVVVVVVVVVVVVVVVVVVVVVVV
VVVVVVVVVVVVVVVVVVVVVVVVVVVVVVVVVVVVVVVVV
VVVVVVVVVVVVVVVVVVVVVVVVVVVVVVVVVVVVVVVVV
VVVVVVVVVVVVVVVVVVVVVVVVVVVVVVVVVVVVVVVVV
VVVVVVVVVVVVVVVVVVVVVVVVVVVVVVVVVVVVVVVVV
VVVVVVVVVVVVVVVVVVVVVVVVVVVVVVVVVVVVVVVVV
VVVVVVVVVVVVVVVVVVVVVVVVVVVVVVVVVVVVVVVVV
VVVVVVVVVVVVVVVVVVVVVVVVVVVVVVVVVVVVVVVVV
VVVVVVVVVVVVVVVVVVVVVVVVVVVVVVVVVVVVVVVVV
VVVVVVVVVVVVVVVVVVVVVVVVVVVVVVVVVVVVVVVVV
VVVVVVVVVVVVVVVVVVVVVVVVVVVVVVVVVVVVVVVVV
VVVVVVVVVV   VVVVVVVVVV
VVVVVVVVVV   VVVVVVVVVV
VVVVVVVVVV   VVVVVVVVVV
VVVVVVVVVV   VVVVVVVVVV
VVVVVVVVVV   VVVVVVVVVV
VVVVVVVVVV   VVVVVVVVVV
VVVVVVVVVVVVVVVVVVVVVVVVVVVVVVVVVVVVVVVVV
VVVVVVVVVVVVVVVVVVVVVVVVVVVVVVVVVVVVVVVVV
VVVVVVVVVVVVVVVVVVVVVVVVVVVVVVVVVVVVVVVVV
VVVVVVVVVVVVVVVVVVVVVVVVVVVVVVVVVVVVVVVVV

N. H. PRITCHARD: "Born in New York City on October 22, 1939, N. H. Pritchard prepared at The Cathedral Choir School of St. John the Divine and St. Peter's School (Jacob's Hill) before receiving his Bachelor of Arts degree with Honors in Art History from Washington Square College, New York University. While attending college, he was a contributor to the literary magazine and President of the Fine Arts Society. Mr. Pritchard pursued graduate studies in Art History at the Institute of Fine Arts and Columbia University. His poems have appeared in numerous periodicals, among them: *Poetry Northwest, Liberator, Eye Magazine, Umbra,* the *East Village Other,* as well as in several anthologies. He has given readings of his poems at many institutions, including International House, Sarah Lawrence College, The Poetry Society of America, Lafayette College, and Barnard College. He has read his poems on the record albums *Destinations: Four Contemporary American Poets* and *New Jazz Poets.* Mr. Pritchard is currently teaching a poetry workshop at the New School for Social Research and is Poet-in-Residence at Friends Seminary."

"Words are ancillary to content"

Lennox Raphael

Mike 65

(1)

Once up u hurl a stone
        thru the window
But coming up the musulmanos laugh
        thru cactus corners

while Mike 65 looks down on sea sun and stones

        and falls upon the city
where the cactii are hungry   and mosquitoes full
        but coming up the musulmanos laugh
        and Mike 65 looks down on the city

(2)

stone upon stone upon stone the mountains are one
And the bird that dies to the loins   really dies

for the loin is   where the head is
        rested in peace

(3)

Once up yr feet sit
The wind breathes for u
The sun washes yr face

and the musulmanos come   in sandals & whistles
                    begging cigarettes
to feed the mad goat   that refuses bread and apple
                    as the dog turns
and the goat returns
mad as the game   that climbs mountains
                    and plants flags on skeletons

while Mike 65 looks down on the city

(4)

The dead had been dead centuries
The fort never stooped to defend the truth
                    the cactus was always sweet
                    the children never laughed
                        so openly
              and on the way down the jasmins were
                    sweet
but the sea lies far and near   out of reach and love
and on the way down the jasmins were sweet

(5)

Mike 65 who cares
Not again   too much
if someone so much as mentions a castle say   SO WHAT
So what, so what!

stay away from hills
that fall upon themselves
in beautiful cities

Surprising then each time the last
But never the end of boasting boasting boasting

Mike 65 to the dozen, a dead bird, the sea, the wind

Surprising then the wind speaks every tongue
                    playing the trees to a harp
and Mike 65 to the dozen
And a bird, the sea, the stones, and the wars lost on the hill

(6)

Examine the flesh
See stone   and more stone

ask yrself: why did the goat refuse bread why the dog afraid why did the bird die
           why did the wars destroy themselves why do people go to hills of mourning

Tear the question from the flesh
And be fed like the rest
Tight in the city

                              where ruins ruin ruins
                              and the young never grow too old
                              to die like the yellow bird

Covered with jasmins and dew

(7)

into another sleep   another death
into the clockhand waving   you're UP
ready
And the city becomes whiter   and whiter
to the resting place of white houses & couscous daughters

And the men are hilled in their animals

And the pleasures are twofold and pleasurable

(8)

is mint sweeter than tea
on the far side of the hill
        where mountains fornicate
        and stones attend sorrow

Where Mike 65 is   scratched on the wall
Where the stone is   hurled at the city
Where the dog is   first to turn back
        smoking new dreams

(9)

The musulmanos smile at the mountains
        climbing over the weary   climbers
And the cactus becomes chumbo becomes a prick of evil
        and the stones roll up their sleeves

Where shepherds slept the musulmanos come
with staff with bag, a smile
smiling on cold rock

And dogs bark off their jaws
And children large over mountains

And when the mountain is humbled
    then shall the people pray
           and the stones will confess

And the jasmins will bloom

    (10)

there is a fly on every mountain
and it romances the only jasmin   until Mike 65
Returns to the source

And thereafter
        and the fly follows the last traveler
        and takes the traveler to bed
        and seduces the traveler
With sugar and tears

    (11)

coming up a stirrup in the sky
going down a dead bird
        and jasmins crisp as butterfly wings
        bathing the dead bird with sweet dreams

as the city spreads into sea river mountain and ruins at our feet

(12)

they were men once   who climbed themselves
                    looking down on the city

                    spread out like the beautiful lay
            and veiled by mountainous cheeks
                    as the harlot returns to her tears

and a heart that like a stallion is broken several places

(13)

            Oh city yr mountains are falling

                                down
And yr dead are buried by moonlight
                                        oh city
            yr cemeteries are grave mistakes
And yr houses are christian nomads
                                oh city
Are u filled every morn with the dew   that
            washes the face of the dead
Are u judge for the bird
                                        that
            sits in jasmins

(14)

Some stones are firmer than the breast
Some roads shorter than the job

But Mike 65 becomes god to the ruins   and devil in time
And the musulmanos   perched on the brow of the city
                    become the mouth
And speak to the bird   praising the jasmins
          and beating their chests

and the bird   seeing a stone fly
asks a lift   and is made whole
as the feet of those who danced on cactii
                    and made petard of stones
                    and sat in windows
                    and caressed the goat
                    and fed dogs
And spake to the dew with the voice of the wind
          as the wind replied
          with a mournful dirge
that goes thru one ear of the city   and become ramparts
                                        and forts
          as the wind becomes silent
          as the stone that only speaks
When thrown at the dead   by the living dead
                    dead as the feet of the climbers
          no longer perched on their fears
no longer at the top   no longer at the top   no longer at the now
no longer a bird   no longer a stone   no longer a voice

alone alone alone   alone as the dead

                    alone as the living dead
          whose jasmins never ripen and love

whose eyes never see the voice of the hills
nor feathers on the stone
that steadies the feet   and quiets the heart
in a cup of water
taken with love

(15)

there are thousands of mountains in the sky
   and the mountain range is the magic darkness
and each foot that goes up is pulled down
& rushed to the dunes
dust of the magic darkness

and the falling bird
falls for the stone
and the hand used is used by the stone

and the bird that flies away
                  becomes more beautiful
and the eye that sees its flight   sees
                  everything

          and becomes the city
and as castle keeps hill   so hill keeps bird
          and each stone is smooth

                  smooth
     as the beak of the dead
                  smooth
     as the crust of jasmins

(16)

and Mike 65 is bee to hive
    as bee as honey can be

but if the castle is noised when the night is white
    say so what
        so what

and jasmins will never fade for love
and mountains will guard the city

and Mike 65 will be bee to the hive

and stones will not fly to sweet thrushes in the voice
and stones will not fly

Nighttime

The night is surrounded   by the sea
And the sea is surrounded
      by an awful stillness
And the lantern perch rides the white wave
      upon a pole star
Which is the captain in white binoculars
Commanding the destroyers. As salt sweeps
      the deck red. With blood
To wash no angel clean.   No lamb dry
To wash no death lean.   No hopes high

The night remains unexplored. As love
Is the stillness of the million
Lonely ones. Who have sought refuge
In the depths of their own silence. Which are
The depths of unfulfilled corpses. That now
Throw up ideas. And yawn a famished order
Into charity. Given up by daughters of the star.

LENNOX RAPHAEL has become known internationally because of his controversial play, *Che*. Born in Trinidad in 1940, he worked as a reporter in Jamaica. His writing has been published in *American Dialogue, Negro Digest*, and *New Black Poetry*. He worked with the Teachers and Writers Collaborative at P.S. 26, Brooklyn, in 1969, and for some time has been on the staff of the *East Village Other*.

Carolyn M. Rodgers

Portrait

mama spent pennies
in uh gallon milk jug
saved pennies
fuh four babies
college educashun

and when the babies
got bigger they would
secretly "borrow" mama's
pennies to buy candy

and pop cause mama
saved extras
fuh college educashuns
and pop and candy

was uh non-credit in bad teeth
mama pooled pennies
in uh gallon milk jug,
Borden's by the way

and the babies went
to school cause mama saved
and spent and paid
fuh four babies

college educashuns
mama spent pennies
                  and nickels
                  and quarters
                  and dollars

and one life.
mama spent her life
in uh gallon milk jug
fuh four black babies
college educashuns.

We Dance Like Ella Riffs

the room was a
red glow, there was
a warm close pulsating.
Chairs and tables were
                          sprawled like a semi-circle
bowing to the band stand where
                              ripples of light lingered
on the silver tracings of player's
soulpieces and
brightened and glistened and
dazzjangled
like tear drops
in a corner
                 suspended
and spit on by the light
                         again and again and oooooh

                              splu dah dee
                              do dah'um dah
                              spleeeeee

the dancers were
soft breezes, smooth
jerky moving
ballooon move the air
no moving was the
wrong moving
roll with the notes
sift through the beats
pause, the music
                    sure carelessly careful, caresses cor-recting the air

we are music
sound & motion imitate us
each of us,
Black variations
                    on a
Round theme
any one
of us—
an infinite, essential note
                    sounding down this world.

The Rain Is in Our Heads

        *to the daughters of Birmingham and to Medgar Emmett
        Martin and Malcolm*

rotting murders are fresh blood clots
        in our brains, daily, daily

we no longer know to care who the winners were—

      the rain is in our heads . . .

oh, and thunder is the rain while the dreams
      inside ourselves
are echoes of shrieking tears
              we did not answer

and at each of our ends
they will claw our robot flesh, wring out our rigid tongues
    crack our glass bodies
              we did not move on time to
the screams they screamed we screamed
fire sirens   screammmmmmmssssss
   riffing in our dreams, that should have
speared our fingers, cannoned our fists into
what need be.
      they screa-mmmmmmed

    they knew.   they need not have died . . .

we look not into our eyes, our eyes, oh
infinite coiling key holes
        red torches in the beginning
blink spinning to a yellowness, to this yellowredness
     that is our
ending/beginning, beginning
        when our flat feet heaved weight

as round metals glassed our bones
       souls to stone

we are stoned soul that will not know a way to save our own
　　the rain is in our heads . . .

we will sip thick plates of blood, bathe in blood, pour blood
　　birth blood, die blood, blood it is and has always
　　　　been/ we are blood come alive
　　　　how dead stoned souls moan

　　　　the rain is in our heads . . .
　　　　the murders are in our minds
　　　　the murders are of our blood
and　　　the blood, the blood is us

until fire burns the rain in our heads . . .

c. c. rider

　　april 16, 1969

carl died last night
　　young
　　talented
　　　　musician.

　　struggling
　　tuh make it
　　tuh be famous
　　　　　　tuh be his dream self

　　　　dealing in them herbs
　　　　droppin pills

more & more
more
when fame didn't happen

not remembering
that the program
only allows for

one
at
uh
time
nowatimes perhaps, no
not
one. yeah uh huh.

carl died
last night
wite folks
sd
it was uh
hem-or-rage
(in the head)

but
weblacks
know
the ways of
genocide.

Plagiarism for a Trite Love Poem

you talked of the sun and moon
while i sat,
supportin my chin with my thumbs
and i thought of two stars, your eyes.
you expounded and pounded,
paced and raved
about fire and ice and the world's certain doom
and i was sure you were warmth,
you spelled out what was wrong with the brothas and
i pretended i understood
            (that's when i noticed your lips)
you explained "the wite boy" your hands shavin the
air as though in uh fight or some crucial hurry
and i silently agreed
then you spoke of the need for Black Unity and
i said yes.
            (and you kept on talkin) and
i said yes.
            (and you paused and listened) and

i
said
yes . . .

U Name This One

let uh revolution come. uh
state of peace is not known to me
anyway

since I grew uhround in chi town
where
howlin wolf howled in the tavern on 47th st.
and muddy waters made u cry the salty nigger blues,
    where pee wee cut Lonnell fuh fuckin wid
    his sistuh and blood baptized the street
    at least twice ev'ry week and judy got
    kicked out grammar school fuh bein pregnant
    and died tryin to ungrow the seed
       we was all up in there and
       just livin was guerilla warfare, yeah.

let uh revolution come.
couldn't be no action like what
      i dun already seen.

Jesus Was Crucified *or*

It Must Be Deep
(an epic pome)

i was sick
and my motha called me
tonight yeah, she did she
sd she was sorri
i was sick, but what
  she wanted tuh tell
me was that i shud pray or
have her (hunky) preacher
pray fuh me. She sd i
had too much hate in me

she sd u know the way yuh think is
got a lots to do
wid the way u feel, and i
agreed, told her i WAS angry a lot THESE days
and maybe my insides was too and she sd
    why it's somethin wrong wid yo mind girl
that's what it is
                and i sd yes, i was aware a lot
lately and she sd if she had evah known educashun
woulda mad me crizi, she woulda neva sent me to
school (college that is)
she sd the way i worked my fingers to the bone in
this white mans factori to make u a de-cent some-
bodi and here u are actin not like decent folks
        talkin bout hatin white folks & revolution
& such and runnin round wid NegroEs
    WHO CURSE IN PUBLIC!!!! (She sd)
THEY COMMUNIST GIRL!!! DON'T YUH KNOW
     THAT???
      DON'T YUH READ*THE NEWSPAPERS?????
                   (and i sd)
i don't believe—(and she sd) U DON'T BELIEVE IN GOD
   NO MO DO U?????
u wusn't raised that way! U gon die and go tuh HELL
and i sd i hoped it wudn't be NO HUNKIES there
and she sd
what do u mean, there is some good white people and some
bad ones, just like there is negroes
and i says i had neva seen ONE (white good that is) but
she sd negroes ain't readi, i knows this and
deep in yo heart you do too and i sd yes u right
negroes ain't readi and she sd
why just the utha day i was in the store and there was
uh negro packin clerk put uh colored woman's ice cream
in her grocery bag widout wun of them "don't melt" bags
  and the colored ladi sd to the colored clerk

"how do u know mah ice cream ain't gon tuh melt befo I
git home."
    clerk sd. "i don't" and took the ice cream
    back out and put it in wun of them "stay hard"
    bags,
and me and that ladi sd see see, ne-groes don't treat
nobody right why that clerk packin groceries was uh
grown main, acted mad. white folks wudn't treat yuh that
way. why when i went tuh the BANK the otha day to de-
posit some MONEY
this white man helped me fast and nice. u gon die girl
and go tuh hell if yuh hate white folks. i sd, me and
my friends could dig it . . . hell, that is
she sd du u pray? i sd sorta when i hear Coltrane and
she sd if yuh read yuh bible it'll show u read genesis
revelation and she couldn't remember the otha chapter
i should read but she sd what was in the bible was
happnin now, fire & all and she sd just cause i didn't
 believe the bible don't make it not true
      (and i sd)
 just cause she believed the bible didn't make it true
and she sd it is it is and deep deep down
in yo heart u know it's true
      (and i sd)
 it must be deeeep

she sd i mon pray fuh u tuh be saved. i sd thank yuh.
 but befo she hung up my motha sd
 well girl, if yuh need me call me
i hope we don't have to straighten the truth out no mo.
i sd i hoped we didn't too
    (it was 10 P.M. when she called)
she sd, i got tuh go so i can git up early tomorrow
and go tuh the social security board to clarify my
record cause i need my money.

work hard for 30 yrs. and they don't want tuh give me
$28.00 once ev'ry two weeks.
       i sd yeah . . .
don't le em nail u wid no technicalities
       git yo checks . . . (then i sd)

    catch yuh later on jesus, i mean motha!

        it must be
            deeeeep . . .

It Is Deep

    (don't never forget the bridge that you crossed over on)

Having tried to use the
witch cord
that erases the stretch of
thirty-three blocks
and tuning in the voice which
    woodenly stated that the
    talk box was "disconnected"

My mother, religiously girdled in
her god, slipped on some love, and
laid on my bell like a truck
blew through my door warm wind from the south
concern making her gruff and tight-lipped
    and scared
that her "baby" was starving,
she, having learned, that disconnection results from non-pay-
    ment of bill(s).

She did not
recognize the poster of the
grand le-roi (al) cat on the wall
had never even seen the book of
Black poems that I have written
thinks that I am under the influence of
       communists
when I talk about Black as anything
other than something ugly to kill it befo it grows
    in any impression she would not be
considered "revelant" or "Black"
                         but
there she was, standing in my room
not loudly condemning that day and
not remembering that I grew hearing her
curse the factory where she "cut uh slave"
and the cheap j-boss wouldn't allow a union,
not remembering that I heard the tears when
they told her a high school diploma was not enough,
and here now, not able to understand, what she had
been forced to deny, still—

she pushed into my kitchen so
she could open my refrigerator to see
what I had to eat, and pressed fifty
bills in my hand saying "pay the talk bill and buy
some food; you got folks who care about you . . ."

My mother, religious-negro, proud of
having waded through a storm, is very obviously,
a sturdy Black bridge that I
crossed over, on.

CAROLYN M. RODGERS was born and raised in Chicago, Illinois, where she now lives. An active member of OBAC (Organization of Black American Culture), she has traveled around the country reading her poetry and lecturing. In 1968 she won the first Conrad Kent Rivers Writing Award. In that year she also taught Afro-American literature at Columbia and at the City College of New York. Her first book of poetry was *Paper Soul*. This was followed by a broadside, *2 Love Raps*, and a 1969 volume, *Songs of a Blackbird*.

"I will write about things that are universal," Carolyn Rodgers has said. This has meant writing about the particulars of life: eating, loving, being born, and dying. While her work revolves around a black experience and while its individuality has a black flavor, it is very much an exploration of the human condition.

Sonia Sanchez

right on: white america

this country might have
been a pio
                neer land
once.
        but.   there ain't
no mo
            indians   blowing
custer's mind
                    with a different
image of america.
                            this country
might have
                needed shoot/
outs/ daily/
                    once.
                            but. there ain't
no mo real/ white   allamerican
                            bad/ guys.
just.
    u & me
            blk/ and un/armed.
this country might have
been a pio
                neer land,   once.
                                    and it still is.

check out
            the falling
gun/shells   on our blk/ tomorrows.

for our lady

yeah.
        billie.   if someone
had loved u like u
shd have been loved
ain't no telling what
kinds of songs
                u wd have swung
against this country's white mind.
or what kinds of lyrics
                wd have pushed us from
our blue/ nites.
                yeah.   billie.
if some blk/ man
                had really
made u feel
                permanently warm.
ain't no telling
                where the jazz of yr/ songs
                wd have led us.

summer words for a sister addict

the first day i shot dope
was on a sunday.
                        i had just come
home from church
                        got mad at my mother
cuz she got mad at me.   u dig?
                        went out. shot up
behind a feeling gainst her.
                                it felt good.
gooder than dooing it.   yeah
                                it was nice.
i did it.   uh. huh.   i did it.   uh. huh.
i want to do it again.   it felt so gooooood.
                        and as the sister
                        sits in her silent/
                        remembered/ high
                        someone leans for
                        ward gently asks her:
                                sister.
                                did u
                                finally
                        learn how to hold yr/ mother?
and the music of the day
                        drifts in the room
to mingle with the sister's young tears.
                        and we all sing.

so this is our revolution

niggers with naturals
still smoking pot drinking
shooting needles into their arms
for some yesterday dreams.
sisters fucking other sisters'
husbands
        cuz the rev o lu tion done
freed them to fight the
enemy (their sisters)
               yeah.
                   the
revo lution   is here
               and we still
where our fathers/
             mothers were
twenty yrs ago
            cept we all look
prettier.
        cmon bros.   sisters.
how bout a fo/
            real/   revolution
with a fo/ real
           battle to be fought
outside of bed/
         room/ minds.
like.   there are children
to be taught to love their blk/ selves
a blk/culture
              to be raised on this
white/ assed/ universe.
           how bout a
fo/ real

sun inspired life
               while
these modern/ day/ missionary/
           moon/ people
go to the moon
              where they belong.

blk/ rhetoric

for Killebrew, Keeby, Icewater, Baker, Gary Adams and Omar Shabazz

who's gonna make all
that beautiful blk/ rhetoric
mean something.
              like
i mean
       who's gonna take
the words
        blk/ is/ beautiful
and make more of it
than blk/ capitalism.
                  u dig?
      i mean
          like who's gonna
take all the young/ long/ haired
natural/ brothers and sisters
and let them
        grow till
           all that is
impt is them
        selves

SONIA SANCHEZ

                    moving in straight/
revolutionary/ lines
                    toward the enemy
(and we know who that is)
                         like. man.
who's gonna give our young
blk/ people new heroes
        (instead of catch/ phrases)
        (instead of cad/ ill/ acs)
        (instead of pimps)
        (instead of white/ whores)
        (instead of drugs)
        (instead of new dances)
        (instead of chit/ ter/ lings)
        (instead of a 35¢ bottle of ripple)
        (instead of quick/ fucks in the hall/ way
          of white/ america's mind)
like.   this.   is an S O S
    me.   calling. . . . .
                        calling. . . . .
                                        some/ one
        pleasereplysoon.

—answer to yr/ question

of am i not yr/ woman

even if u went on shit again—

& i a beginner
            in yr/ love
say no.

SONIA SANCHEZ

      i wd not be yr/ woman
& see u disappear
              each day
befo my eyes
          and know yr/
reappearance
        to be
           a one/
               nite/ stand.
no man.
     blk/
     lovers   cannot   live
in white powder that removes
them from their blk/ selves
                 cannot ride
majestic/ white/ horses
          in a machine age.
blk/ lovers
       must live/
      . . . . . . push against the
devils of this world
         against the creeping
whiteness of their own minds.
i am yr/ woman
        my man.
          and blk/ women
deal in babies and
        sweet/ blk/ kisses
and nites that
      multiply by twos.

indianapolis / summer / 1969 / poem

like.
    i mean.
        doesn't it all come down
to e/ co/ no/ mics.
          like.   it is for
money that those young brothers on
illinois &
      ohio sts
         allow them selves to
be picked up
       cruised around
          till their
asses open in tune
       to holy rec/ tum/
            dom.
& like. ain't it
     fo coins
        that those blond/
wigged/ tight/ pants/
       wearing/ sisters
open their legs/ mouths/ asses
       for white/ dicks
to come
   in tune to
      there ain't no
asses
  like blk/ asses.
      u dig?
and i mean.
    like if brothers
programmed sisters for love
instead of
   fucking/hood

                    and i mean
if mothers programmed
                    sisters for
good feelings bout their blk/ men
and i
        mean if blk/ fathers proved
their man/ hood by
                    fighting the enemy
instead of fucking every available sister.
and i mean
            if we programmed/
                        loved/ each
other in com/ mun/ al ways
                    so that no
blk/ person starved
                or killed
                        each other on
a sat/ ur/ day nite corner.
then. may
        be   it wd all
come down to some
                    thing else
like RE VO LU TION.
                i mean if.
                        like.
yeah.

Sonia Sanchez was born in 1935 in Birmingham, Alabama. She studied at New York University and at Hunter College where she received a B.A. in 1955. Recently, she taught creative writing at San Francisco State College. At present, she is living in Pittsburgh and is married to Ethridge Knight, like her a poet widely published in magazines and anthologies.

The poetry of Sonia Sanchez uses the language of the everyday black world, of the Harlems throughout the country. It is full of that world, including the realities of dope addiction, discrimination, instability, hostility, and yearning. Her concern and identification are so intense that she is bitter at the self-destructive impulses of her soul brothers and soul sisters inasmuch as she knows and declares that these are the marks of oppression. What she feels about black people, and it would seem about people generally, comes through in her poem to Billie Holiday when she says (in a different context), "if someone/ had loved u like u/ shd have been loved/ ain't no telling what/ kinds of song/ u wd have swung . . ."

Askia Muhammad Touré

JuJu

for John Coltrane, Priest-prophet
of the Black Nation

The Opening
(From the Chronicle)

". . . and They were there in the City of Fire, enflamed,
Their souls burnin' and a'thirstin' for the Light—
the Rain, the Water of the Soul, extinguished by
the Long Whiplash of the Dead.
And They cried out to God to deliver them, or send
a bit of Light from Eternity to let Them know that
He really cared, still cared.
So He sent Geniuses, Magic Men of Old:
Scientists and Prophets, Scholars and Sages,
Philosophers and Myth-making Priests.
Garvey and DuBois, Langston and Booker T.,
Bessie and Satchmo, Bird and Lady Day,
Malcolm and Elijah, Otis and Aretha—
and John Coltrane.
And this Last, this is his Testament, his Requiem, his
dues-payin' Eulogy: John Coltrane . . ."

The Pain

Tone. Blue skies and flowing fountains.
Flowering spring-trees, trees, away from here now,
this blooming inwardly as the Soul flows and grows
to newer vistas higher than before.
This journey to the Source of love, garden in the core
of life, tone, this ever-aching loneliness or need
to meet the matchless rhythms of the heart.

Take him now heart and soul of Life—essence wonder
blowing wind of love-change and sounds of Blackness
born of Mother Earth.
Tone. Brown and ebon hue shackled with the matchless
chains of Time. Born blood born tone of dripping
screaming sheets of sound, born bleeding with the
dripping wound of Lash and shrieking mindless pain
grown silent with the flow of silent years.

Down trash-blown streets among the tragic mass of shrunken
twisted shells of warriors wine-soaked, dope-bent Blackmen
once proud seed of pulsing loins thrilling to
the touch of Summer rain.

Take him! Take him! to your wombs, to your bosoms
Mothers, Harlem! Africa!—
strong and vibrant with your love.
He Priest Prophet Warrior call and Clarion Call
of essence—US, BLACKNESS—as in Eastern swan-tone
cry of pale towers falling, burning in the bitter
Fires of Change.

Or Eric in Paris, pain growing madly from his genius heart
like strange flowers of our ever-present death.
Death here, death there; they go from us, all giants:
MALCOLM! ERIC! OTIS! LANGSTON!—
now the Prophet Warrior Priest of Blackness: TRANE!
go TRANE go TRANE away in essence of blue-sky tone
hunger Black loneliness of nightdeath calling
through Eastern regions of the Heart:
                                    TRANE! TRANE! TRANE!

The Joy

Down vistas of light I hear him call me, my
brother magic piper of
                        Visions of Now.
His horn cascading fountains of blood and bones and stormy
rainbows firedarts purple blue-song tear-stained
channels of love.
Past green beast-eyes and the carnal leer of lust and hate
we wander sad in our soul-song, big as life and warm
as throbbing Earth loamy in the crystal rain of Spring.

We, poet and magic myth-making Giant of Song, wander on.
Holy the bones of our ancestors wrapped in Pyramids
        resting till the end of Time.
Holy the Magi, priests and Myth-scientists of Africa
        for sending him to us.
He with Eternity upon his horn cascading diamonds of Destiny
to our blues-ridden hearts crushed against the Towers
        of the West.
O Magic! to live dynamic in the Soul against the deadly
concrete and steel blaring trumpets—Hell gazing from
        the blue killer-eyes.

Solo   Solo   Solo   for Africanic joys: rhythm thrilling from
the mobile hips of choclit mamas Bird-of-Paradise pagan colors
Joy vibrating from the rat-nests of the West.
And greens and cornbread, sweet potatoes boogalooing
        in the brilliance of his smile.

PRAISE BE TO:
                    Africa, Mother of the Sphinx,
who brought our souls back from the Land
                            of the Dead.

PRAISE BE TO:
                    the Old Ones:
Magi in pyramidal silence who
made the JuJu in our blood outlast
the Frankenstein of the West.

PRAISE BE TO:
                    Thutmose and Hermes
    Piankhi and Nefertari
                    Songhai
            and Dahomey—
                        Ghana and Benin

laugh with purple gums, nigger lips, shiny teeth
at the resurrection of their seed amid
gunfire in the Harlems of the West.

PRAISE BE TO:
                    ALLAH
who brought us Malcolm and Elijah
and reopened Islam like a Flaming Torch
to elevate our souls and send us
soaring to the mountains of the Black World
seeking Paradise.

137

And through it all the echoes of his horn
blowing Joy thrilling golden fountains Love and Beauty
flowing Spring and dark witch-eyes, full nigger-lips,
wooly hair like Dionne/ 'Retha singing us to Blackness
sprouting from our genes sprouting in the wine-flush
of our blood to course into our full-expanding Minds
and lift us high upon a hill above the ghetto death-traps
past Suffering and Want past Heartbreak and Heartache to
      Eternity and God—and he is
NOT gone for I can see, can hear him still: my Heart
      my Soul my All vibrating—TRANE!

> *"A LOVE   SUPREME*
> *A LOVE   SUPREME*
> *A LOVE   SUPREME*
> *A LOVE   SUPREME*
> *A LOVE   SUPREME*
> *A LOVE   SUPREME*
> *A LOVE   SUPREME . . . ."*

Pome for Dionne Warwick aboard the aircraft carrier *U.S.S. Enterprise*

"ENTERTAINING" TROOPS!

Damn! . . . Baby, when I saw all of that warmth,
that life, that joy
sucked in by the savage eyes of Beasts
raining "democratic" death upon the yellow world
of Vietnam, I almost cried.
YOU!—decked out in gaudy mod colors,

mini-skirt riding high above regal honey thighs,
raped by the Dollar Juggernaut—"ENTERTAINING"
   TROOPS!"
Soulsister,
Black Princess chained upon the *Modern Auction Block*,
listen while the Auctioneer shouts above my rage:
    "BID

        'EM

           IN! ! ! "

Tauhid

for Pharaoh Sanders and
the youth of the Black Nation

Reach like you never reached before past Night's somber robes
into the star-crossed plains of Destiny.
Reach with hungry Black minds towards that bright Crescent
   Moon
glowing in the depths of Malcolm's eyes.
Stranded within the coils of this most Evil of centuries,
holy with Change bursting from your spirit's loins,
reach the Sun of Nature's prophets: Ancient Magic
singing us to Love, Eternal Beauty Cosmic Rhythms flowing
in the sound of Pharaoh's horn.
Reach past the death in your mama's religion—centuries lost
in the veil of jewish eyes—into the throbbing heart of
Africa flowing into Mecca, warm undulating blood vibrating
   Truth
implanting JuJu in your mind above the plaster-death of zombies
rotting in the madhouse of the West.

139

Reach into the Womb of Time, past aeons of chains,
to find your Afro-Soul, that holy part of you connecting Harlem
to the roots of Timbuktu.
In this last great Voyage, walk togetha children, take my hand
Sister-Brother, take my heart my wisdom take, turn this Wheel
to Cosmic Order: Allah's Love vibrating in the Sunrise burning-
ghetto-winds-of-Freedom blowing, Angels calling *Sunrise!*
    Lovers
Warriors *Daybreak!* Dreamers, reach the mountain of your
    Rebirth
in the Whirlwind of our Rising in the West!

"Askia Muhammad Abu Bakr el-Touré: Servant of Allah, rev-
olutionaray activist, Magi of the Black Nation. Poet-essayist.
Editor-at-Large of the *Journal of Black Poetry*, Contributing
Editor of *Black Theater* magazine. Works have appeared in a
number of publications, including *Liberator, Soulbook, Negro
Digest, Black Dialogue, Freedomways, Asia, Africa, Latin
America Revolution*, and the anthologies *Black Arts* and *Black
Fire*."

"Calling Mankind, calling Third World Brothers, calling Man-
kind, calling Third World Brothers, calling Mankind, calling
Black people, calling Black people, calling Brown people, call-
ing Yellow people, calling Yellow people, calling Third World
Brothers, calling Third World Brothers:
    The Sun Is Rising In The West!
    The Sun Is Rising In The West!
    The Black Nation Is Rising/ The Black Nation Is Rising
    The Black Nation in the Dead/Cracker/West is Rising
    shaking the foundations of the EvilCrackerEmpire
    (GOG & MAGOG)!
"WE are its voices, WE are its magic singers, shamans, proph-
ets, beyond this limited evil Now, we work Spiritual JuJu upon
his twisted soul (GOG & MAGOG): singing his children into
hippies, singing him to CANCERHEARTDISEASE, ASHES
& HONKIEDEATH.
"WE conjure up a future, reaching into our Afro-Souls, into
the spiritual realms of our Afro-Manity, calling forth the blood
& spiritual energies of departed Ancestors: lost African Souls
screeeeaaaaming in Middle Passage Death, Slave-revolt leaders,
castrated warriors, raped mothers, lynch-rope victims of "lib-
erty." From our Towers in the West, WE invoke the Whirl-
wind of Revolution, causing the planet to shake upon its moor-
ings. WE invoke Apocalypse to purge this plant of Evil & the
White Lie. But beyond this, beyond the blood & flames of
Armageddon, WE invoke new visions of ORIGINAL MAN/

SPIRITUAL MAN/COMMUNAL MAN, evolved to harmony with his brothers & the Universe, Master of Nature, Lover of Peace. New Visions of full bellies/ hope-filled eyes/ disease-free bodies/ liberated minds & spirits. It will be—yes! We WILL do it here/now—yes! Beyond cracker-ism and white magic in the alienatedpresentevilNow—yes! BlackMusicMagic Vision here/now—yes! CitiesBurningHonkies dyingEvilFading here/now—yes! WE WILL WIN/WE WILL WIN/WE WILL WIN/WE WILL WIN/WE WILL WIN/WE WILL WIN/WE WILL WIN—YES! Calling Mankind, Calling Third World Brothers, Calling Mankind, Calling Third World Brothers, Calling Mankind . . ."

Tom Weatherly

arroyo

tallest poet for his height
hang up he projectd th body
on th page. jig &
real poems unrolld off his knuckles
in tall black
neighbor hoods
faces down on him
down wif pearly
mother cohen spinning willam jim crow
jane in th morning. me tarzan.

crazy what she calls

it's much harder to treat a woman
than it is to treat a man.
we are allowed to mix piss in th toilet
thot we had to be married for that, but no
one will care, even if we declare our unmarriage,
marriage fuckn our heads, together, apart
more than when we ate 3 breakfasts in th hip bagel.
i was th rapist but you were th villain, white
rumanian jew, samuels—didnt your family change

its name? marshmallow mattress on a putty frame.
you thot who was that tall dark handsome stranger.
Hmmmmmm
bullshitter.
hey thats not a street light thats th moon.

for billie

a dyke can't
hold back th sea
boyish finger stuck in
or boy's will, it's her flesh
she can't hold back.

loony tune.

pool doos paid

mudcat shango, his black pitch
attitude in state of grace
in th heart of th mountain.

lion seidel, devil grin on
off fightn th lower
heaven expressway.

ishmael reeds bony mushrooms
shitface on moonseed
spookn coloured greens black dyed peas.

peachtree payne swishd
how it was wif catfish gravy,
acoustical blue guitar.

. . .

& we spent out our honeymoon
on calle espana, old san juan tours
paved wif anvil petals. lil tomcat
shootn his shit in your veins
varicose tracks in your legs.

out of scorpio & pisces
fuckd his way out of your pussy
                                    is awake now
this hard dick morning for me
th lil mothersucker won't even leave
corners in your tits.
                        he's th balance
of our days. you lookn like a grandmom
pinch his foreskin—

we will die venerable   my pretty.

mud water shango

a big muddy daddy my daddys gris-gris to the world.
i'm a big muddy daddy daddys gris-gris to the world.
got a mojo chop for sweet black belt girl.

daddys a river & my mamas shore is black.
daddy a river mamas shore is black.
flood coming mama you cant keep it back.

lightning in my eyes mama thunder in your soul.
theres lightning in my eyes mama thunder in your soul.
i'm a river hip daddy mama dig a muddy hole.

red & yellow fooles coat

a bouquet for my lady

yellow ladys
bedstraw. white ladys bedstraw.
3 faces under a hood.
love in a mist. smoke of the earth.
old mans beard. devil in a bush.

wild madder. sun spurge.
good night at noon.

violet-coloured bottle. egyptian
lotus water. phisick spurge.

blue for franks wooten

House of the Lifting of the Head

let me open mama your 3 corner box.
yes open mama your 3 corner box.
i have a black snake baby his tongues hot.

146

you shake round those curves baby dont quite make the grade.
you shake round those curves baby dont make the grade.
man come home tired dont want no lemonade.

we been blowing spit bubbles baby in each others mouf.
we been blowing spit bubbles baby in each others mouf.
burst all them bubbles mama norf cold like the souf.

let me be your woodpecker mama tom do like no pecker would.
let me be your woodpecker mama tom tom do like no pecker
    would.
open your front door baby black dark come home for good.

speculum oris

for sam

bladderwort. blue
frog in th harbour street

bird leg nora
a mo bile bama
high strut heels about
wif her pig fat ass

spiked thighs open
to th scramble

in Jong sang doo
, 'nor charged God foolishly.'

Tom Weatherly:
"tomcat born on railroad
avenue, scottsboro, alabama
to big tom & lucy belle
weatherly, november 3, 1942

"dad in european theatre
mom & i living
wif his mom & dad

"after the war dad & mom & lil sis & i
moved to the mountain
street home. grade & high school
at george washington carver, split
off to morehouse college at the end of
eleventh grade.

"two & half years at morehouse
semester at alabama a.&m.
then parris island
& dante's inferno, another semester
at normal, alabama, made Q frat sic
wif bundle of sticks in hand.
indefinitely suspended from a.&m.
for publishing The Saint on campus
without permission.

                    "had a vision
entered a.m.e. ministry
assistant pastor of saint pauls scottsboro
disciple of saint/j. c. coleman
& next year pastor of church great granddad
pastored (bishop i. h. bonner had feel for tradition).

"had a division: left god mother hooded youth &
the country for new york, lived on streets,
parks, hitchd the states.
                              dishwasher at hip bagel,
waiter in the mountains, cook at lion's head,
proofreading copyediting, baking, bellhopping,
camp counselor, dealing, fuckd up in the head.
rantd in the saint marks poetry project, ranting
now in afrohispanic poets workshop east harlem.

"HOLDER OF THE DOUBLE MOJO HAND & 13TH
DEGREE GRIS-GRIS BLACK BELT."

Publications: *Maumau American Cantos*, Corinth, 1970
Contributor to: *The World, The Grub, For Now, 3C 147,
UTTER, Simbolo Oscuro, Cuchulainn, Extensions, The World
Anthology, Excalibur.*

Jay Wright

An Invitation to Madison County

I ride through Queens,
out to International Airport,
on my way to Jackson, Tougaloo, Mississippi.
I take out a notebook,
write "my southern journal," and the date.
I write something,
but can't get down the apprehension,
the strangeness, the uncertainty
of zipping in over the Sunday streets,
with the bank clock flashing the weather
and time, as if it were a lighthouse
and the crab-like cars mistook it
for their own destination.
The air terminal looks
like a city walled in, waiting for war.
The arrivals go down to the basement,
recruits waking at five AM to check out their gear,
to be introduced to the business end of the camp.
Fifteen minutes in the city,
and nothing has happened.
No one has asked me to move over
for a small parade of pale women,
or called me nigger, or asked me where I'm from.
Sure only of my destination, I wait.

Now, we move out through the quiet city,
past clean brick supermarkets,
past clean brick houses with nameplates
and bushy lawns, past the sleepy-eyed
travelers, locked tightly in their cars.
No one speaks. The accent I've been
waiting to hear is still far off,
still only part of that apprehension
I had on the highway, in Queens.

The small campus springs up
out of the brown environment,
half-green, half-brown, covered over
with scaly white wooden houses.
It seems to be fighting this atmosphere,
fighting to bring some beauty
out of the dirt roads, the tense isolation of this place.

Out to Mama's T's, where farmers, young instructors
and students scream for hamburgers and beer,
rub each other in the light of the jukebox,
and talk, and talk. I am still
not in Jackson, not in Mississippi,
still not off that highway in Queens,
nor totally out of Harlem, still
have not made it into this place,
where the tables creak, and the crickets
close up Sunday, just at evening,
and people are saying goodnight early.
Afraid now, I wonder how I'll get into it,
how I can make my hosts forget
these impatient gestures, the matching socks and tie
I wonder how long I'll have to listen
to make them feel I listen, wonder
what I can say that will say,
"It's all right. I don't understand

a thing. Let me meet you here, in your home.
Teach me what you know,
for I think I'm coming home."

Then I meet a teen-aged girl,
who knows that I can read.
I ride with her to Madison County,
up backroads that stretch
with half-fulfilled crops,
half-filled houses, half-satisfied
cows, and horses, and dogs.
She does all the talking,
challenging me to name the trees,
the plants, the cities in Mississippi, her dog.
We reach her house,
a shack dominated by an old stove,
with its smoky outline going up the wall
into the Mississippi air, mattresses tossed
around the table, where a small piece of cornbread
and a steaming plate of greens wait for her.
Her mother comes out, hands folded before her
like a madonna. She speaks to me,
moving step by step back into the house,
asking me to come again,
as if I were dismissed,
as if there were nothing more
that I could want from her, from Madison County,
no secret that I could ask her to repeat,
not even ask about the baby resting there on her belly,
nor if she ever knew anyone with my name
in Madison County, in Mississippi.

Since I can't, and will not, move,
she stays, with her head coming up,
finally, in a defiant smile.
She watches me sniff the greens,

look around at the bare trees
heaving up out of the bare ground.
She watches my surprise
as I look at her manly nine-year-old
drive a tractor through the fields.
I think of how she is preparing him
for death, how one day he'll pack
whatever clothes remain from the generations,
and go off down the road,
her champion, her soldier, her lovable boy,
her grief, into Jackson, and away,
past that lighthouse clock,
past the sleepy streets,
and come up screaming,
perhaps on the highway in Queens,
thinking that he'll find me,
the poet with matching socks and tie,
who will tell him all about the city,
who will drink with him in a bar
where lives are crackling, with the smell
of muddy-rooted bare trees, half-sick cows
and simmering greens still in his nose.

But I'm still not here,
still can't ask any easy question,
or comment on the boy, the bright girl,
the open fields, the smell of the greens;
can't even say, yes, I remember this,
or heard of it, or want to know it;
can't apologize for my clean pages,
or assert that I must change, after being here;
can't say that I'm after spirits in Mississippi,
that I've given up my apprehension
about pale and neatly dressed couples
speeding past the lighthouse clock,
silently going home to their own apprehensions;

can't say, yes, you're what I really came for,
you, your scaly hands, your proud, surreptitious
smile, your commanding glance at your son,
that's what I do not search, but discover.

I stand in Madison County,
where you buy your clothes, your bread,
your very life, from hardline politicians,
where the inessential cotton still comes up
as if it were king, and belonged to you,
where the only escape is down that road,
with your slim baggage, into war,
into some other town that smells the same,
into a relative's crowded house
in some uncertain city, into the arms
of poets, who would be burned,
who would wake in the Mississippi rain,
listening for your apprehension,
standing at the window in different shadows,
finally able to say, "I don't understand.
But I would be taught your strength."

The father comes down the road,
among his harness bells and dust,
straight and even, slowly, as if each step
on that hard ground were precious.
He passes with a nod,
and stands at the door of his house,
making a final, brief inventory
all around and in it.
His wife goes in, comes out with a spoon,
hands it to you with a gracious little nod,
and says, "Such as . . ."

"Such as . . . ," as I heard
when my mother invited the preacher in,

or some old bum, who had fallen off
a box-car into our small town
and come looking for bread-crumbs,
a soup bowl of dish water beans,
a glass of tap water, served up
in a murky glass.
"Such as . . . ," as I heard
when I would walk across the tracks
in Bisbee, or Tucson, or El Paso, or Santa Fe,
bleeding behind the eyes,
cursing the slim-butted waitresses
who could be so polite.
"Such as . . . ," as I heard
when I was invited behind leaky doors,
into leaky rooms, for my loneliness,
for my hunger, for my blackness.
"Such as . . . ," as I hear
when people, who have only themselves to give,
offer you their meal.

Moving to Wake at Six

I never wake at six,
though I lie,
wrapped to my scalp,
twirled like a mummy in my clothes,
with my ears awake to a bus
singing bass in the hills.
Though I am still not awake,
I turn and catch the white shadows
leaning at my door like drugstore cowboys.
I hear everything that moves,

or would move.
I seem myself to have split
and moved to every corner of the town,
watching jeweled vegetables drop
and float on the floor of the market,
standing on the moldy arch of the bridge,
watching a man uncurl from the braids
of a fat woman, and roll his mat,
and there, at the governor's gate,
where two soldiers march,
smug and tight as clam shells,
to hang the flag in a wisp of sun.
The town is changing voices,
changing faces, moving from one
life to another, and I am still
at that point of choosing to move
and wake, or fall off again,
one of those who cannot scurry
to the solemn cluck of a clock,
one who cannot give up
the frightening warmth of shroud-like clothes,
where perhaps I could wake,
under a tinted window,
to conjure up a glazed lake,
a bearded man and a boy,
and a vision that could be my own.

The Homecoming Singer

The plane tilts in to Nashville,
coming over the green lights
like a toy train skipping past
the signals on a track.
The city is livid with lights,
as if the weight of all the people
shooting down her arteries
had inflamed them.
It's Friday night,
and people are home for the homecomings.
As I come into the terminal,
a young black man, in a vested gray suit,
paces in the florid Tennessee air,
breaks into a run like a halfback
in open field, going past the delirious faces,
past the poster of Molly Bee,
in her shiny chaps, her hips tilted forward
where the guns would be, her legs set,
as if she would run, as if she were
a cheerleader who doffs her guns
on Saturday afternoon and careens
down the sidelines after some broken field runner,
who carries it in, for now,
for all the state of Tennessee
with its nut smelling trees,
its stolid little stone walls
set out under thick blankets of leaves,
its crisp lights dangling on the porches
of homes that top the graveled driveways,
where people who cannot yodel or yell
putter in the grave October afternoons,
waiting for Saturday night and the lights
that spatter on Molly Bee's silver chaps.

I don't want to think of them,
or even of the broken field runner in the terminal,
still looking for his girl, his pocket
full of dates and parties, as I come
into this Friday night of homecomings
and hobble over the highway in a taxi
that has its radio tuned to country music.
I come up to the campus,
with a large wreath jutting up
under the elegant dormitories,
where one girl sits looking down at the shrieking cars,
as the lights go out, one by one, around her
and the laughter drifts off, rising, rising,
as if it would take flight away
from the livid arteries of Nashville.
Now in sleep, I leave my brass-headed bed,
and see her enter with tall singers,
they in African shirts, she in a robe.
She sits, among them, as a golden lance
catches her, suddenly chubby, with soft lips
and unhurried eyes, quite still in the movement
around her, waiting, as the other voices fade,
as the movement stops, and starts to sing,
her voice moving up from its tart entrance
until it swings as freely
as an ecstatic dancer's foot,
rises and plays among the windows
as it would with angels and falls,
almost visible, to return to her,
and leave her shaking with the tears
I'm ashamed to release, and leave her
twisting there on that stool with my shame
for the livid arteries, the flat Saturdays,
the inhuman homecomings of Nashville.
I kneel before her. She strokes my hair,
as softly as she would a cat's head

158

and goes on singing, her voice shifting
and bringing up the Carolina calls,
the waterboy, the railroad cutter, the jailed,
the condemned, all that had been forgotten
on this night of homecomings, all
that had been misplaced in those livid arteries.
She finishes, and leaves,
her shy head tilted and wrinkled,
in the green-tinged lights of the still campus.
I close my eyes and listen,
as she goes out to sing this city home.

Wednesday Night Prayer Meeting

On Wednesday night,
the church still opens at seven,
and the boys and girls have to come in
from their flirting games of tag,
with the prayers they've memorized,
the hymns they have to start.
Some will even go down front,
with funky bibles,
to read verses from Luke,
where Jesus triumphs, or Revelations,
where we all come to no good end.
Outside, the pagan kids
scramble in the darkness,
kissing each other with a sly humility,
or urinating boldly against the trees.
The older people linger
in the freshly lit night,
not in a hurry to enter,

having been in the battle of voices
far too long, knowing that the night
will stretch and end only
when some new voice rises
in ecstasy, or deceit, only
when some arrogant youth
comes cringing down front,
screaming about sin, begging
the indifferent faced women
for a hand, for a touch,
for a kiss, for help,
for forgiveness, for being young
and untouched by the grace
of pain, innocent of the insoluble
mysteries of being black
and sinned against, black
and sinning in the compliant cities.
What do the young know
about some corpulent theologian,
sitting under his lamp,
his clammy face wet,
his stomach trying to give up
the taste of a moderate wine,
kissing God away with a labored
toss of his pen?
How would these small black singers
know which Jesus is riding
there over the pulpit,
in the folds of the banner
left over from Sunday,
where the winners were the ones
who came, who dropped their nickels
into the felted platters with a flourish?
And how can they be expected
to remember the cadences
that will come again,

the same heart-rending release
of the same pain, as the clock turns
toward the certainty
of melancholic afternoons,
roast and left-over prayers,
the dampened hours that last through the night?
But Christ will come,
feeling injured, having gone
where beds were busy without him,
having seen pimps cane their number running boys,
the televisions flicker over heaped up bodies,
having heard some disheveled man
shout down an empty street, where women
slither in plastic boots, toward light,
their eyes dilated and empty;
will come like a tired workman
and sit on a creaky bench,
in hope, in fear, wanting to be pleased again,
so anxious that his hands move,
his head tilts for any lost accent
He seems to be home,
where he's always been.
His intense smile is fixed
to the rhythm of hands,
to the unhurried intensity
of this improvised singing.
He seems not to know
the danger of being here,
among these lonely singers,
in the middle of a war
of spirits who will not wait for him,
who cannot take his intense glare
to heart anymore, who cannot justify
the Wednesday nights given up
in these stuffy, tilted rooms,
while the work piles up for Thursday,

and the dogs mope around empty garbage pails,
and the swingers swing into the night
with a different ecstasy.
Caught in this unlovely music,
he spills to the floor.
The sisters circle him,
and their hands leap from bone to bone,
as if their touch would change him,
would make him see
the crooked lights like stars.
The bible-reading boy tags him with verses,
and he writhes like a boy
giving up stolen kisses,
the free play of his hand on his own body,
the unholy clarity of his worldly speech.
He writhes as if he would be black,
on Wednesday, under the uncompromising
need of old black men and women,
who know that pain is what
you carry in the mind,
in the solemn memory of small triumphs,
that you get, here,
as the master of your pain.
He stands up to sing,
but a young girl,
getting up from the mourner's bench,
tosses her head in a wail.
The women rise,
the men collect the banners
and the boys drop their eyes,
listening to the unearthly wind
whisper to the peeping-tom trees.
This is the end of the night,
and he has not come there yet,
has not made it into the stillness
of himself, or the flagrant uncertainty

of all these other singers.
They have taken his strangeness,
and given it back, the way a lover
will return the rings and letters
of a lover that hurts him.
They have closed their night
with what certainty they could,
unwilling to change their freedom for a god.

The Invention of a Garden

I'm looking out of the window,
from the second floor,
into a half-eaten patio,
where the bugs dance deliriously
and the flowers sniff at bits of life.
I touch my burned-out throat,
with an ache to thrust
my fingers to the bone,
run them through the wet
underpinnings of my skin,
in the thick blood, around
the craggèd vertebrae.
I have dreamed of armored insects,
taking flight through my stomach wall
the fissured skin refusing to close,
or bleed, but gaping
like the gory lips of an oyster,
stout and inviting, clefts of flesh
rising like the taut membrane of a drum,
threatening to explode and spill
the pent-up desires I hide.

163

Two or three birds
invent a garden,
he said,
and I have made a bath
to warm the intrepid robins
that glitter where the sun
deserts the stones.
They come, and splash, matter-of-factly,
and lonely as sandpipers
at the crest of a wave.
Could I believe in the loneliness
of beaches, where sand crabs
duck camouflaged in holes,
and devitalized shrubs and shells
come up to capture the shore?
More, than in this garrisoned room,
where this pencil scratches
in the ruled-off lines,
making the only sound
that will contain the taut,
unopened drum that beats the dance
for bugs and garden-creating birds.

JAY WRIGHT: "I was born in Albuquerque, New Mexico, May 25, 1935. I played professional baseball with Mexicali in the Arizona-Texas League and with Fresno in the California State League; attended the University of New Mexico (in chemistry) for two months; then spent three years in the army medical corps. I graduated from the University of California (Berkeley) with a B.A. in 1961; spent one semester at Union Theological Seminary in 1961–62; took an M.A. from Rutgers University (New Brunswick, N.J.), in Comparative Literature, in 1966. I tutored in S.A.V.E. in Harlem, read in the Academy of American Poets Schools Program, was a consultant for the Central Atlantic Regional Educational Laboratory in Washington and for the Teachers-Writers Collaborative in New York, went on the Woodrow Wilson–National Endowment Poets-in-Concert tour through the South in 1967. I was poet-in-residence at Tougaloo College (Mississippi) in December, 1968, and at Talladega College (Alabama), fall 1969–70. I've had two writing grants—an MCA Creative Writing Fellowship in 1963 and a National Endowment for the Arts Grant in 1968. I have a Hodder Fellowship as a playwright beginning in September, 1970.

"I've published poems in: *New Negro Poets: USA, New Republic, Poetry Review* (London), *Yale Review, Poetry Northwest, New American Review, Evergreen Review, 31 New Americans Poets, Hiram Poetry Review, Hanging Loose, The Nation, Negro Digest, The Outsider, American Weave, Religious Humanism, Union Seminary Quarterly, Aphid, For Malcolm,* and *Black Fire.* I'll have poems in *Hiram, Hanging Loose, Umbra, Journal of the New African Literature,* and *Arts and Poetry Northwest.* I've also read at the Poetry Center, on BBC, at Wellesley, and at Livingston College, Rutgers. I've had two short plays produced—*The Doors* at Exodus Coffee House in San Pedro, California, and *Welcome, Black Boy* at Playwright's Workshop, University of California (Berkeley)—and one published—*Balloons,* by Baker's Plays. Two short radio plays—*The Death of Mr. Parker* and *The Woman With the Charm*—are being done by KPFA, Berkeley. I've got four long, unpublished, unproduced plays—*Prophets and Fools, Death as History, The Final Celebration*, and *Leon Nadeau's Fortunate Fall*—and, of course, my unpublished book of poems, *Idiotic and Politic*. I'm working on my fifth play which seems to be one part of a two part project. After these, I'll go back to the characters and situation of *Death as History* and do a play carrying that action forward.

"Most of what I'm doing is 'in process' and I'm reluctant to make any more statements about poetry, having done enough of that in the South and on tour. I have an essay coming in the Francis Fergusson festschrift and one in *New American Review*, which would give some idea of my direction. I've been working on the idea that the grounds of myth, history, and art are similar, if not the same. At the moment, I'm trying to carry these investigations into perception and epistemology. As I go, I try to discover how to use these investigations artistically, dramatically. I'm not very far along in them, and I'm afraid that anything I say about what I'm doing, at this point, would make sense only to me. It may even be irrelevant to other writers. This isn't much of a statement, which only means that I haven't got a concrete one, self-transcendent or universal, as the scholars would say, to make, yet."

Al Young

The Song Turning Back into Itself

(Fragment)

Ocean Springs Missippy
you dont know about that
unless youve died in magnolia
tripped across the Gulf
& come alive again
or fallen in the ocean
lapping up light
like the sun digging
into the scruffy palm leaves
fanning the almighty trains
huffing it choo-choo
straight up our street
morning noon & nighttrain
squalling that moan
like a big ass blues man
smoking up the sunset

Consider the little house
of sunken wood
in the dusty street
where my father would
cut his fingers
up to his ankles

in fragrant coils
of lumber shavings
the backyard of nowhere

Consider nazis & crackers
on the same stage
splitting the bill

Affix it all to
my memory of Ma
& her love of bananas
the light flashing
in & out of our lives
lived 25¢ at a time
when pecans was in season
or the crab & shrimps
was plentiful enough
for the fishermens
to give away for gumbo
for a soft hullo
if you as a woman
had the sun in your voice
the wind over your shoulder
blowing the right way
at just that moment in history

Lonesome in the Country

How much of me is sandwiches radio beer?
How much pizza traffic & neon messages?
I take thoughtful journeys to supermarkets,
philosophize about the newest good movie,

camp out at magazine racks & on floors,
catch humanity leering back in laundromats,
invent shortcuts by the quarter hour

There's meaning to all this itemization
& I'd do well to look for it in woodpiles
or in hills & springs or trees in the woods
instead of staying in the shack all the time
imagining too much
                    falling asleep in old chairs

All that childhood I spent in farmhouses
& still cant tell one bush from another—
Straight wilderness would wipe me out
faster than cancer from cigarette smoke

Meantime my friends are out all day long
stomping thru the woods all big-eyed
& that's me walking the road afternoons
head in a book
                    all that hilly sweetness wasting

Everywhere

"You are more beautiful
than sky or sea"
   —Blaise Cendrars

The apples are still as sweet
as the loquats are plentiful
& the breeze thru both trees
sings promises to me
that the sky reinforces

Like sailors of old
I too am amply tattoo'd
with pictures from a journey
thru a life the yogis say
I myself quite consciously chose

before returning to this planet
to work out hassles
Ive sometimes evaded evenings
with a tilt of the beercan
or the clicking on of music

Inside my skin I am intact
striving to be sweeter to the taste
than apple or loquat or wind
itself. My goals havent changed.
Charles Mingus said, "Youve probably

written the same way for a million years."
My heart is more tattoo'd than skin
but the wrinkles you see & white hairs
are designs, records, roadmaps
into a region vaster & deeper than

Marlboro Country, an orchard
where harvest isnt always sweet,
a funnytime land of suns & moons
whose only citizen gets lost enough
to signal irreverently for help

Malagueña Salerosa

For Roberto Mates & for Doris

What beautiful eyes you have there
underneath your own two eyebrows
underneath your own two eyebrows
what beautiful eyes you have there

That's Mexican for O youre too much!
—always loved that mariachi song,
learned it on the Three Star Bus
runs out of ratty Tijuana on out
thru dusty Sonora where they stop you
for no reason to search your bags
as if to ask that you promise you wont
do poems about simply what happens,
on up to Michoacán my green Indian dream
to the top of it all Mexico D.F.

Then one night in the big city
Bob & I were happy & fantastic
tripping up Calle Shakespeare
bourgeois part of town with maids,
arm in arm with joyous Doris
stuck on her NYC politician lover,
Bob brooding his Havana heaven,
me so sad for my only California,
we molest a *macho* a jitterbug—

"How far's it from here to Yucatán?"
"Ay hombre as far as I am dronk!"
—only so much kinder in Spanish spoken

Then the 4 of us arms all linked
walked all the way to quiet Michelet
to serenade young lady D. goodnight

This Mexico City's vanished,
Bob's back in Detroit working welfare,
Doris whoever she was is no more,
there isnt any such jitterbug drunk,
the me of then is gone forever

Good thing the song's still around

The Kiss

Mayakovsky was right
the brass of my tuba does blacken
& I oompah & twist down nights
even the best female poets
couldnt brighten with song,
a quiet dog barking distantly
my only excuse for being alive
so late past 12 by taxi
horn & radio in the rain
finally having made it
to the middle of nowhere
toes aching from the walk
but fingers intact & head
quite nicely on some other planet
where there're no tempting images
to soften the Indian in me,
no sudden left turns or halts
on roads not marked for traffic,

my women human beings being human
who touch my body with a silence
more beautiful than poetry

There Is a Sadness

There is a sadness to this world

There is a grimness
a nastiness in the throat
a foulness of breath
a slackening of the penis into sorrow
a chill in the bloodstream that hurts
—limitations of fleshhood!
   pain of becoming!
In a spasm of forgetfulness
the seed is sown

There is a ragged edge of my life
a shabby contour
rounding down into nowhere,
the rainyness of wanting
I might well have known
wrestling by the woodstove
in Red Clay Mississippi

There is a tumbling
from noplace to noplace
& there is a crumbling
from nothing to zero,
a journey from germ to germ again
in which the soul travels nowhere

There is such thing as soul,
I have felt & can feel it moving
inside myself & others
inspite of ourselves,
the stolen landscapes we frequent
the caverns of doubt in which we hide

There is such thing as life
& it is not this bleak intermission
during which I scurry for bread & lodging
or judge myself by my failures

O there is a shadowy side of my house
where old dreams smoulder
where longings go up in smoke
where a cold & ugly opposite of love
is burning under the sun

Ponce De León / a Morning Walk

You too if you work hard enough
can end up being the name of a street
in a drowsy little Indian town
a day's drive from Mexico City
where orphans like bold Joselito
hustle in the taxi burro streets,
where cosmetic fragrances mingle
with scents of ripe & overripe fruits
& vegetables, where the smell of break-
fast & dinner are almost the same.

The natural odor of dung & bodysweat
rises from the zócalo into a sky, semi-
industrialized, housing the spirits of
blue señoritas with sun soaking into
their rain-washed skirts folded older
& dustier than red or green pepper—
sun of pineapple! Papaya light!

While a crazy rooster's crowing late
a brown baby delights in orange & yellow
balloons floating up like laughter
to tenement windows where a whole family
of older kids wave happy soap wands
that yield fat bubbles part air part
water part light that pop in the
prickly faces of straw behatted gents
rambling by below, ragged & alive—

One morning's moment in this ageless
stone thoroughfare named after just one
dead Spaniard who wanted to live forever.

Dear Old Stockholm

Of course it is snowing
but two city girls, one blonde the other black-
haired, are preparing for bed
in a warm apartment they share.

One is washing her hair
in the bathroom sink
while the other does her hatha yoga exercises.

They have been dancing
with some young men—
one of them from Pittsburgh
(Crawford's Grill
up on the Hill)
& the other from Leamington, Ontario
—who spoke nothing but North American english.

Suddenly, recalling the evening,
the rushing from taxis up inside music clubs,
all of them pleased that it should be so,
the bathroom blonde who,
like a great many Scandinavians
played some instrument in secondary school,
whistles John Coltrane's whole solo
from the Miles Davis "Dear Old Stockholm"
which was an old Swedish folk song.
In fluorescent abandon & in time
she is massaging her foamy scalp with delight.

Hearing all this, the young blackhaired woman
—tensed in a shoulderstand,
head full of blood,
filling with new breath—
is overcome with unexpected happiness.

Both girls smile in private
at the joyfulness of the evening
& at the music & the men, wishing
that it would never end

The Curative Powers of Silence

Suddenly
I touch upon wordlessness,
I who have watched Cheryl
the blind young woman
who lives up the street
out walking at night
when she thinks no one's looking
deliberately heading
into hedges & trees
to touch them & seemingly
to also be kissed,
thus are we each
hugged & kissed,
kissed in daylight,
licked in a fog

Wordless
I fill up
listening for nothing
for nothing at all

as when in life (so-
called) I am set
shivering with warmth
by a child-like vision
of the Cheryl in me
(when I think no one's looking)
plopped in a field
of feathery grass
under watchful trees
letting the pre-mind dream
of nothing at all
nothing at all,

no flicker
no shadow
no voice
no cry,

not even dreaming

—being dreamed

Friday the Twelfth

Floating thru morning
    I arrive at afternoon

to see the bright lightness
    light ness
    of it all

& thank God
& go on living
taking spoiled strawberries
or tapioca pudding gone bad
    out the ice box
my wife likes to fix things
    or buy them
    & put them
    where theyre promptly forgotten

Must wash my hair
    & go get it cut off my head
    head itches

178

notice my luck changes
    when Ive had
    a hair cut
same as if I dont rise before noon
the day doesnt go right

Afternoon becomes evening becomes night

There're worlds into worlds between all worlds
    so dont worry
    about divisions of day
for even when I fall out asleep the day
    wont have ended
    wont have begun

In fact years whoosh by in time for me
    to see myself as endless fool child
& to learn better
    than to laugh at such conditions

Now I bathe & go out into the streets
    airplane raging overhead
    (your head perhaps)
    reminding me how
    even floating must come to an end

"AL YOUNG was born May 31, 1939, at Ocean Springs, Mississippi. He grew up near there and in Detroit. He was educated at the University of Michigan and the University of California at Berkeley. He has traveled widely throughout the United States, Mexico, and Europe, and has worked at a number of occupations: janitor, lab aide, warehouseman, yardclerk for the Southern Pacific Railroad, medical photographer, employment claims assistant, disc jockey, professional musician. He has taught writing for the Neighborhood Youth Corps, the San Francisco Museum of Art Teenage Workshop Project, and at Stanford University where he is presently Jones Lecturer in Creative Writing. He was awarded a Stegner Writing Fellowship in 1966, and his first book of poems (*Dancing*, Corinth Books) received the Joseph Henry Jackson Award in 1969. His stories, essays, and poems have appeared in innumerable quarterlies and little magazines both in this country and abroad. In 1970 Holt, Rinehart & Winston brought out his novel *Snakes*."

"In April of 1965 I enjoyed the first of a remarkable and continuing series of (non-drug-induced) mystical experiences that I consider, thus far, to be the high points of my life. I no longer feel compelled, as I once did, to speak of these experiences directly. I have learned quite painfully that most people are not especially eager to hear of such things, and many, in fact, feel threatened or frightened by them.

"Nevertheless, since the mid-sixties I have been nourished by these intense and blissful interludes and, hence, have drawn much of my inspiration to write and many of my personal notions about poetics from what could be termed religious sources. I am not, of course, referring to church religion. Sometimes there is a vastness I feel growing within me that I could explore and delight in forever. No mere church could contain it. I cannot help but believe that all men have sensed this beautiful endlessness about themselves at one time or another.

It is what I call soul. Occasionally it flowers from me gratui-
tously in the form of a poem.

"The Roland Kirk Spirit Choir sings of 'Music that makes us
cry/ Love that money can't buy/ Let's all search for the reason
why.' * For me the writing of poetry is a spiritual activity.
Poetry should be a music of love: song, a dance, the joyously
heartbreaking flight of the human spirit through inner and outer
space in search of itself.

"The poem, when it is for-real, expands us to the level of our
quintessential selves where we are nothing but spirit and light.
It is, therefore, functional. It serves a purpose in the very
highest sense. All so-called primitive peoples make little or no
distinction between what we call artistic expression and ritual
worship. We need poetry and the love that it imparts as much,
if not more, than we need food, clothing, and shelter.

"We are all lonely and crying and obviously in need of one
another.

"I write and read the writings of others in order that I might
touch and be touched in meaningful and lasting ways."

---

* Roland Kirk: *Volunteered Slavery*, Atlantic LP (SD 1534).